CONTENTS

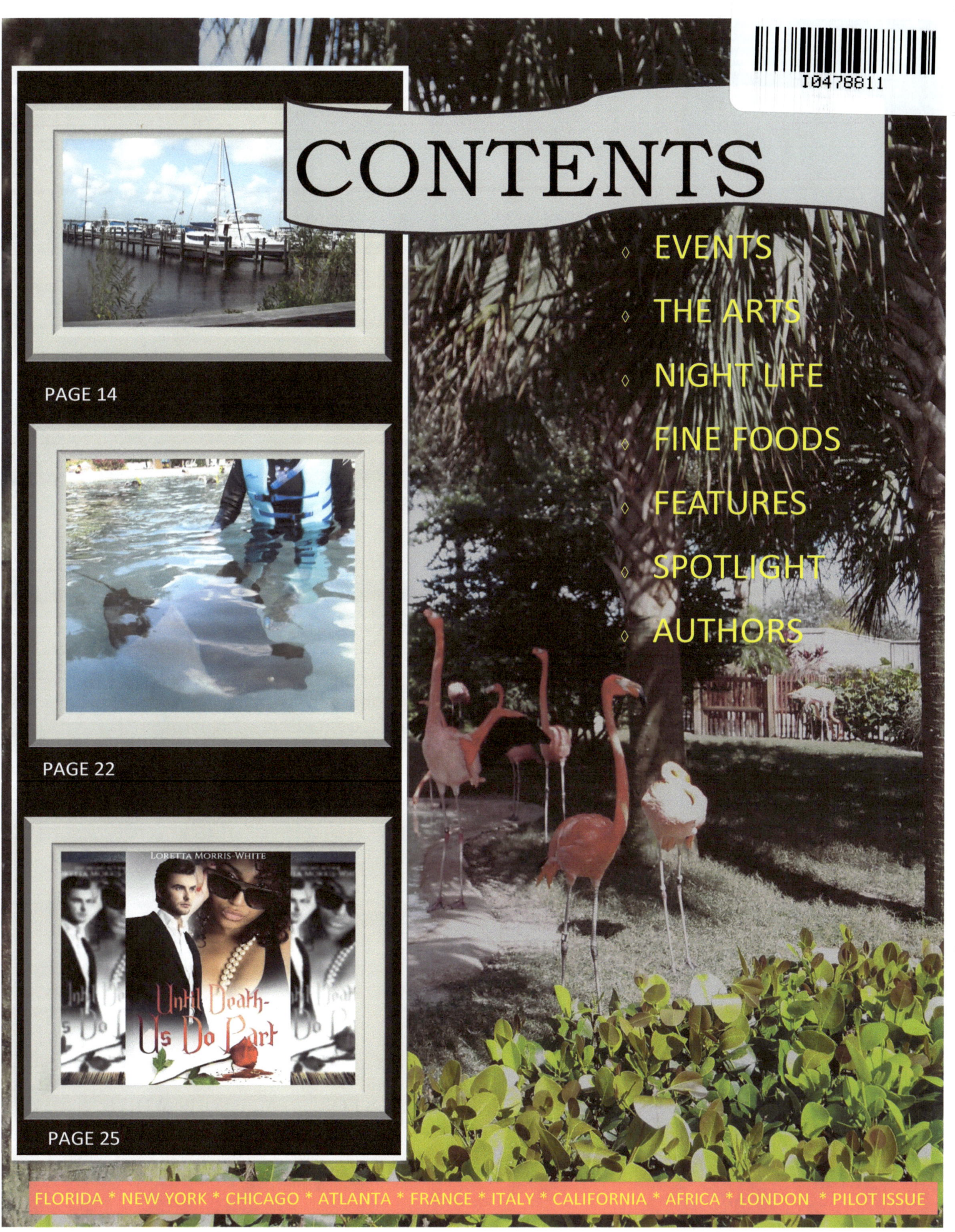

◊ EVENTS

◊ THE ARTS

◊ NIGHT LIFE

◊ FINE FOODS

◊ FEATURES

◊ SPOTLIGHT

◊ AUTHORS

FLORIDA * NEW YORK * CHICAGO * ATLANTA * FRANCE * ITALY * CALIFORNIA * AFRICA * LONDON * PILOT ISSUE

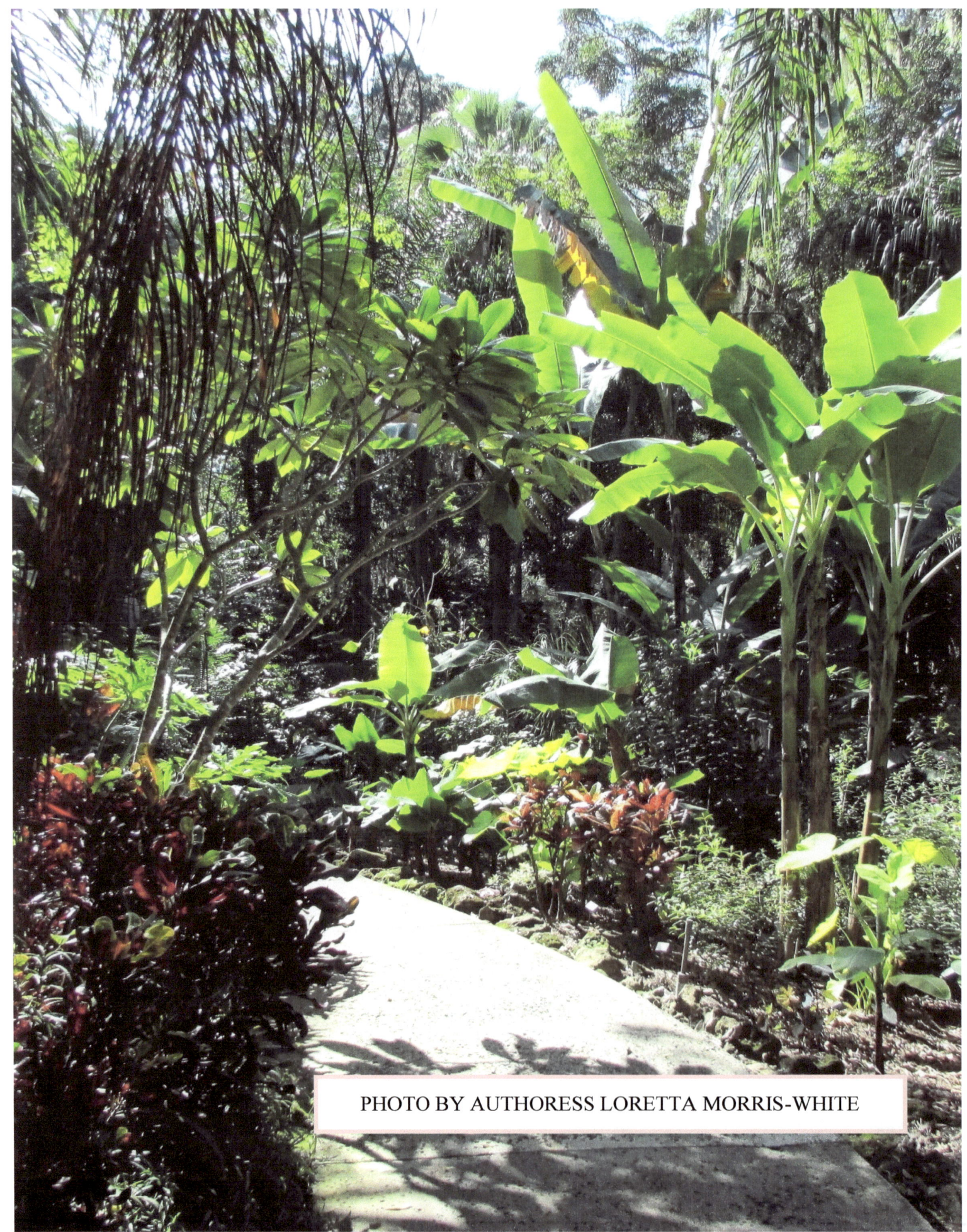

PHOTO BY AUTHORESS LORETTA MORRIS-WHITE

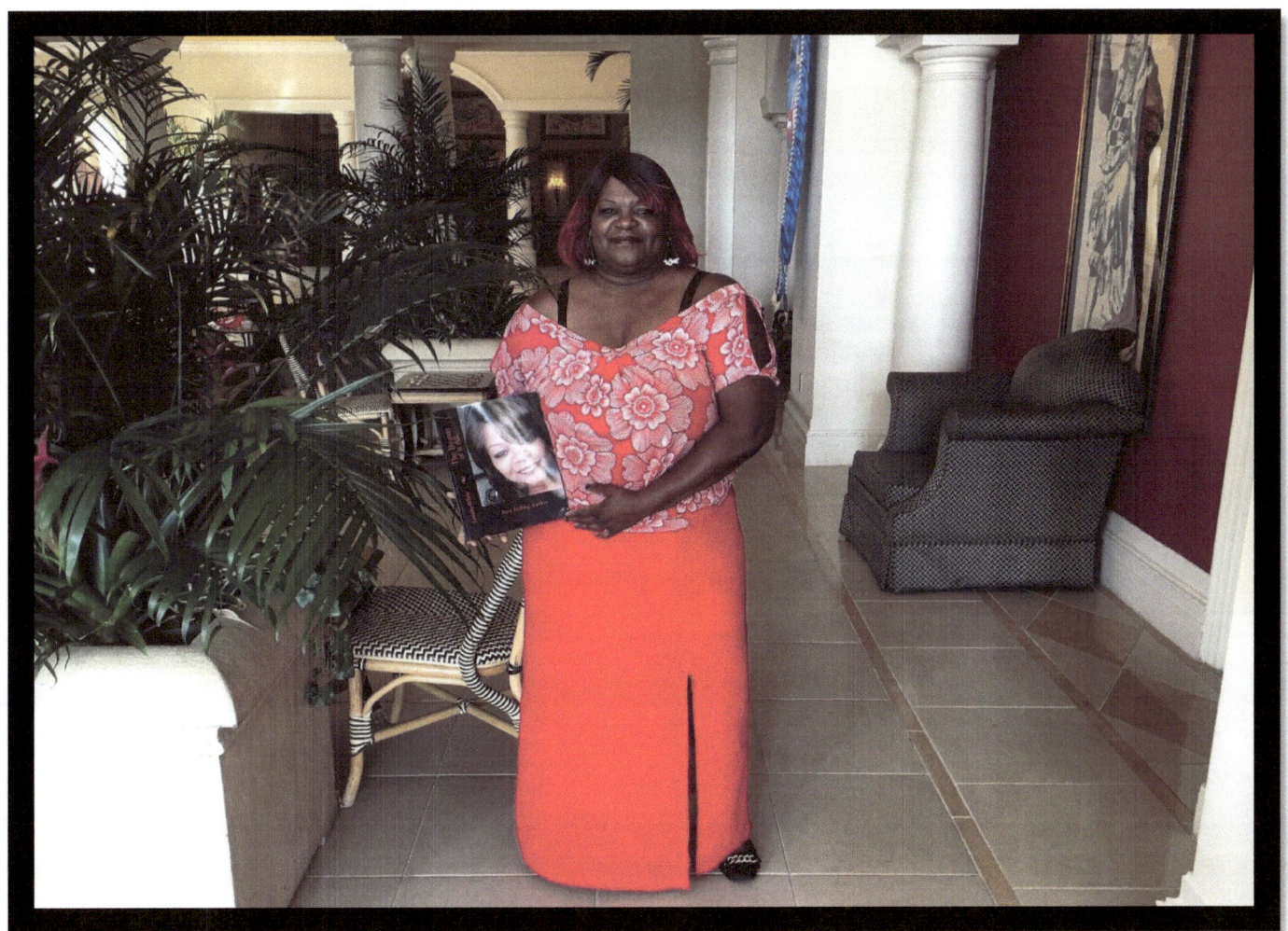

Greetings!

Please join me on a new journey... A Jazzy, Classy and Artistic life-style.

I would like to welcome you to my world of Art. I am an avid lover of the finer things in life. I have always wanted my very own Art Gallery. The reason is for me to just sit and stare into the works of other creative minds. Art consist of many things, there is fashion, hair styling, painting, sculptures, well I might as well say the fine and performing arts. Music is a great way that some express their art as well. Me, I express myself through my Authorship. I love to write. I also love connecting with other writers and providing a platform to present their works as well. Here is a place to do just that. Whatever your Art form may be...Please checkout my website and social media sites to learn more about opportunities and to find out what's happening in the world of the Artz. This magazine has been developed to provide a platform in any form for a business or individual. I feel others should just enjoy ALL beauty.

Again, Welcome

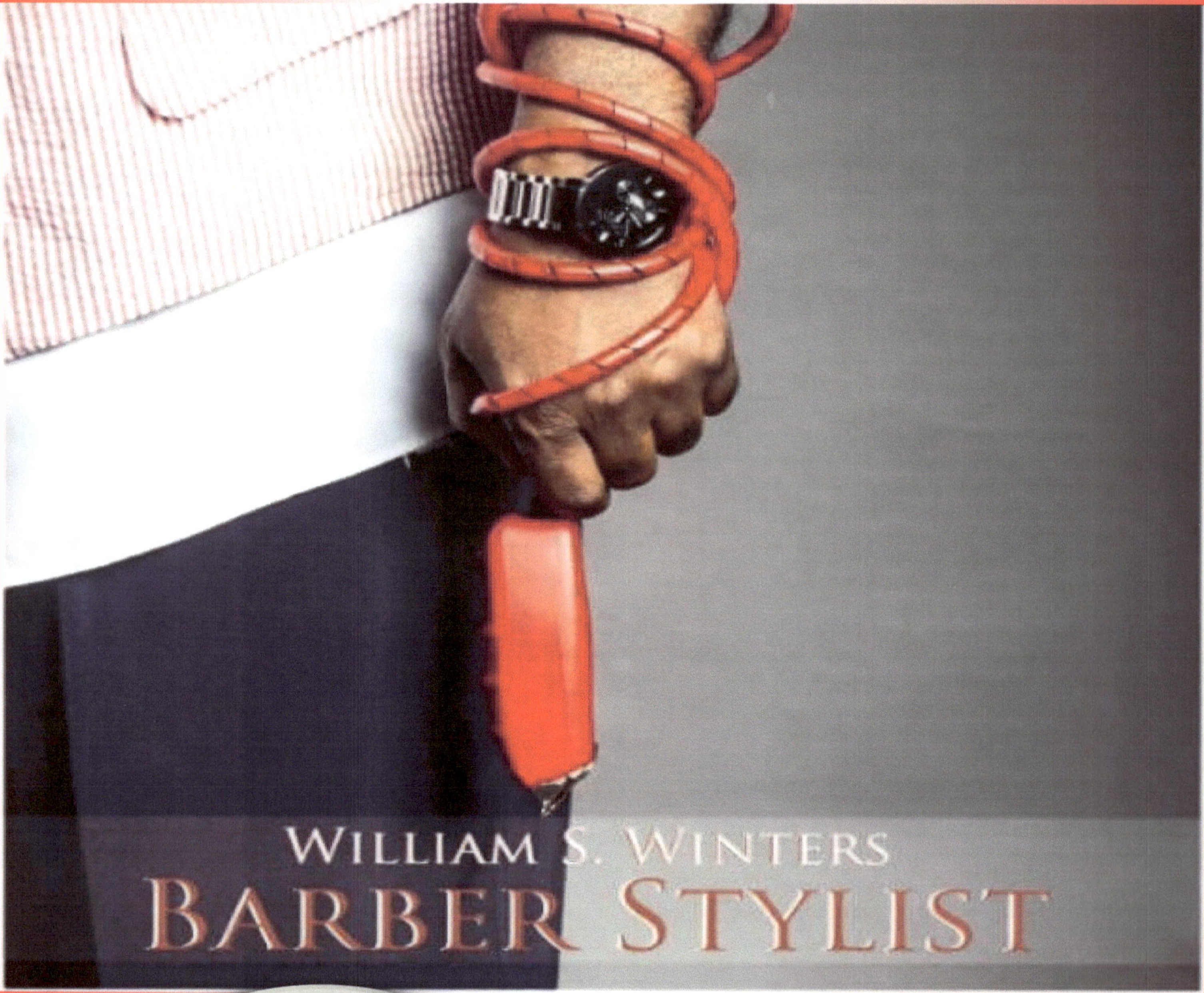

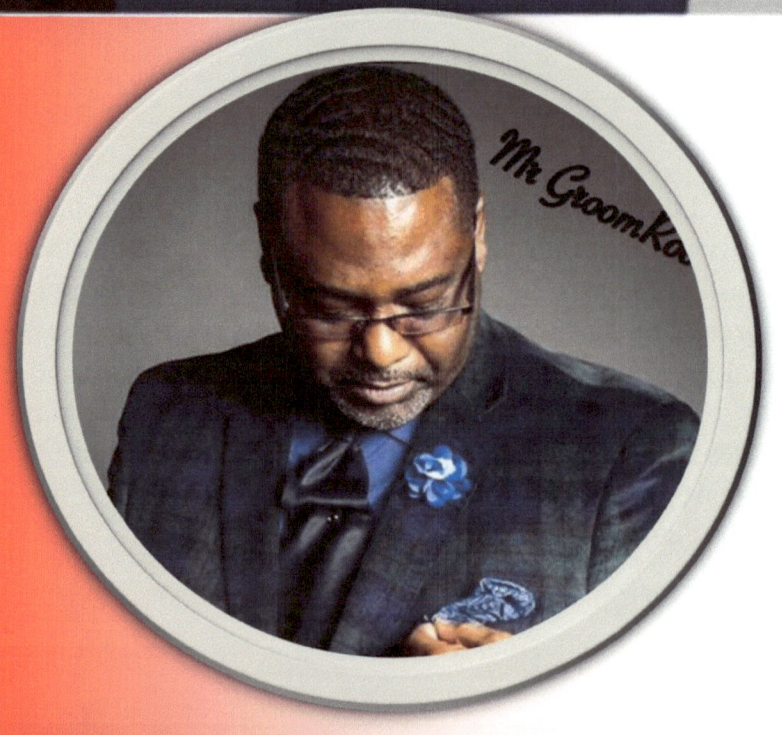

WILLIAM S. WINTERS
BARBER STYLIST

Mr GroomKo

PAGE 5

READ ALL ABOUT

MR. WINTERS

A RALEIGH, N.C.

BARBER AND FASHION GURU.

STYLE IS HIS ART

MEN * WOMEN & CHILDREN HAIR

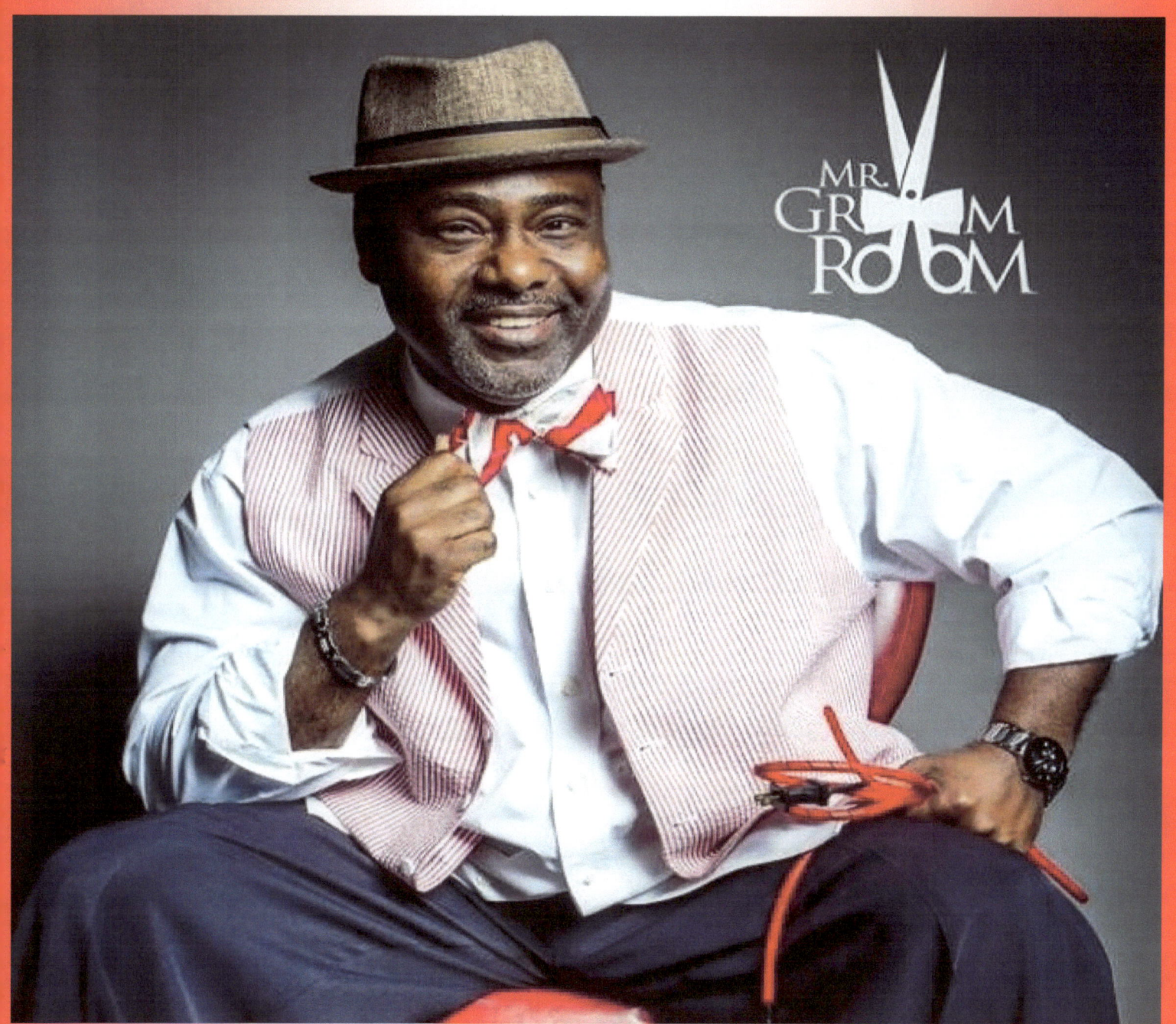

MR. WINTERS IS A MASTER BARBER FROM RALEIGH, NC. HE HAS BEEN CUTTING HAIR FOR 25 YEARS NOW AND STILL SAYS HE HAS A LOT TO LEARN. HE GETS HIS INSPIRATION FROM THE YOUNGER GENERATION DUE TO THE NEW TRENDS THAT ARE COMING OUT EVERY DAY. ONE HAS TO KEEP ABREAST ON EVERYTHING IN THE INDUSTRY TO STAY A FACTOR IN THIS BUSINESS. I STARTED CUTTING HAIR AFTER GOING TO A BARBER SCHOOL YEARS AGO AND GOT TIRED OF THEM CUTTING HAIR ONLY ONE WAY, CUTTING HAIR IS AN ART THAT GOES BACK AS FAR AS B.C. AND BARBERS THESE DAYS ARE NOT TAKING THEIR CRAFT SERIOUSLY, HENCE THE NAME, MR. GROOMROOM. I WANT TO BRING THE ART OF GROOMING AND FASHION BACK INTO THIS INDUSTRY. YOUR BARBER DOESN'T HAVE TO LOOK ANY KIND OF WAY; WE ARE PROFESSIONALS AND SHOULD DRESS AND ACT A PART. WE ARE NO DIFFERENT THAN YOUR LAWYER OR DOCTOR. WHEN YOU SCHEDULE A VISIT TO YOUR LAWYER, HE IS NOT IN HIS OFFICE IN A PAIR OF JEANS, SO WHY SHOULD WE DRESS ANY KIND OF WAY? WE ARE PROFESSIONALS ALSO. I JUST ADD A LITTLE EXTRA FLAVOR TO THE PART.

$\mathcal{M}$R. GROOM ROOM HAS A GOAL TO HOPEFULLY RUB OFF. THE ART OF GROOMING YOUR CLIENT WITH A LITTLE STYLE AND FLAIR. AS A BARBER, MOST OF THE TIME THEY ARE THE LIMELIGHT IN THEIR COMMUNITY. WE ARE YOUR THERAPIST, COUNSELOR, FASHION COORDINATOR AND SOMETIMES MARRIAGE COUNSELOR. LET'S START ACTING AND DRESSING LIKE A PROFESSIONAL AND IT WILL ATTRACT A LOT MORE CLIENTS INTO YOUR CHAIR.

HE WOULD LOVE FOR MR. GROOMROOM TO BE A BIG FRANCHISE IN THE FUTURE. HE HAS ATTRACTED A MANY CLIENTS REINVENTING HIMSELF AND HE IS NOT GOING TO STOP THERE.

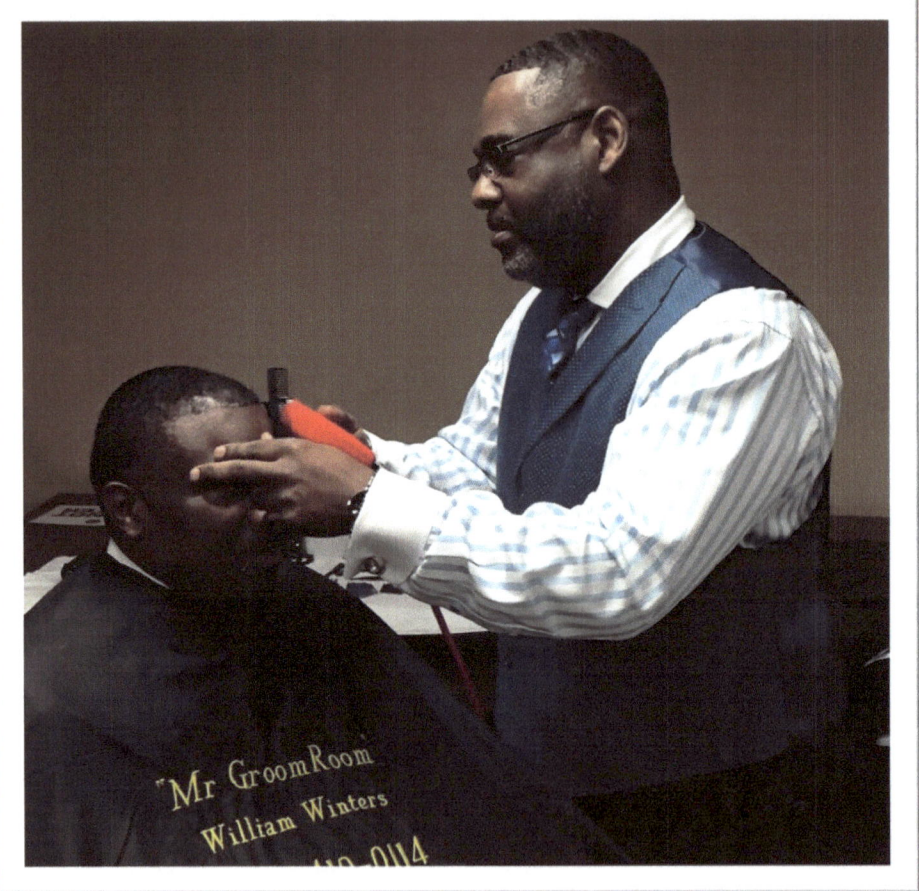

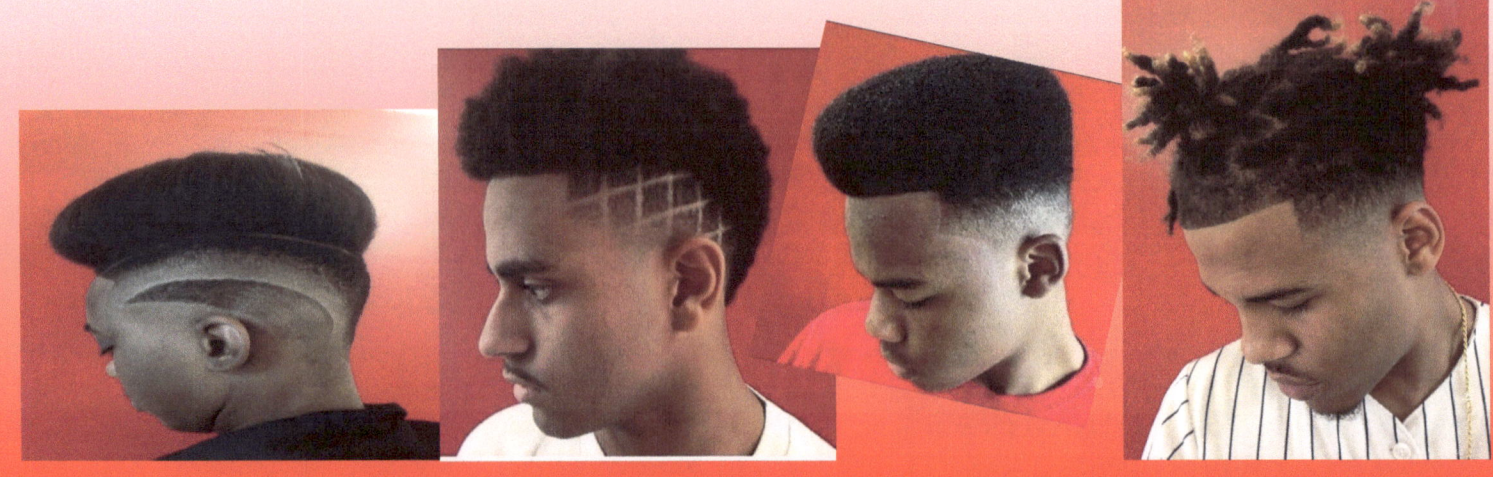

FASHION IS ... ART

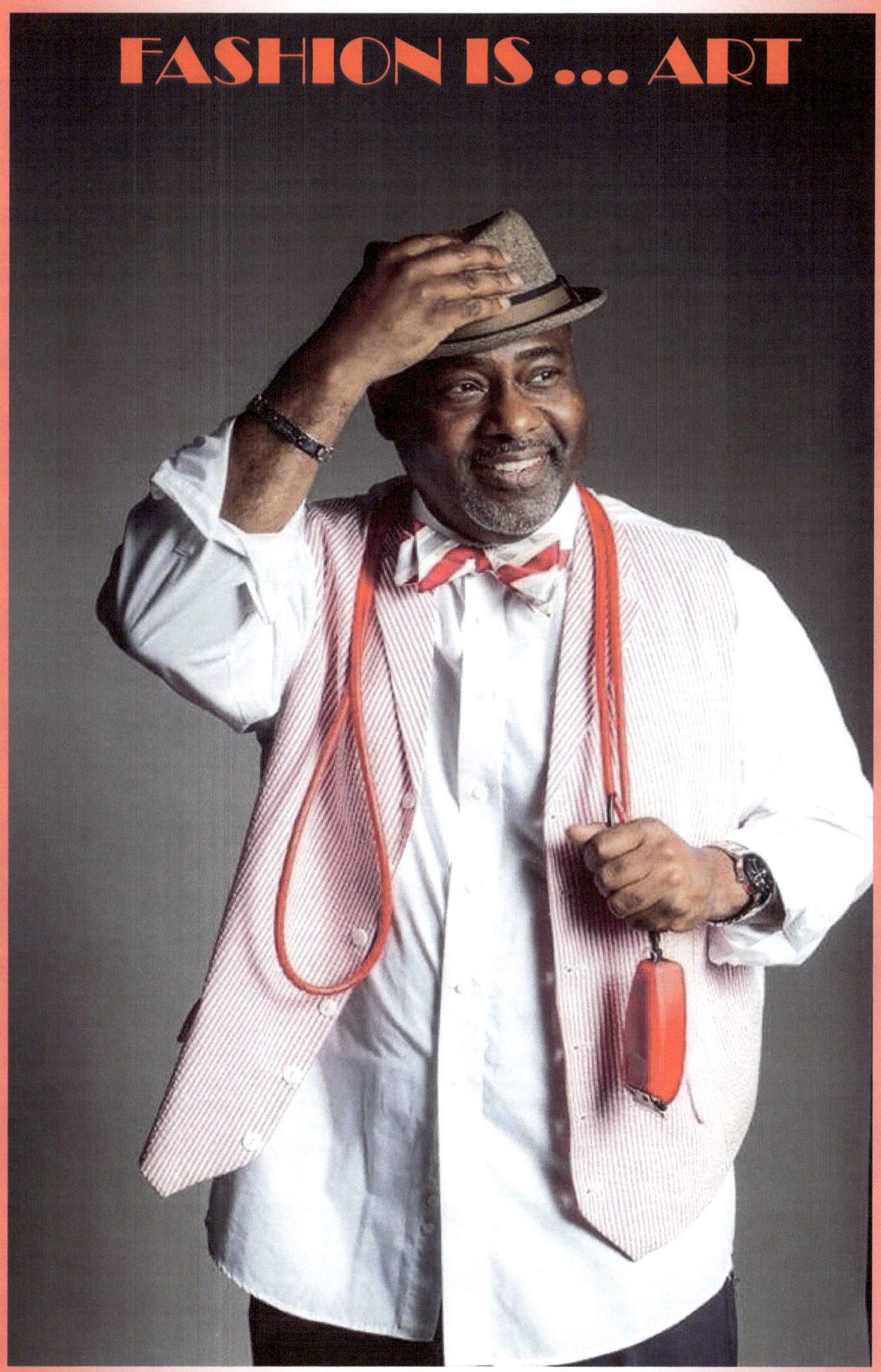

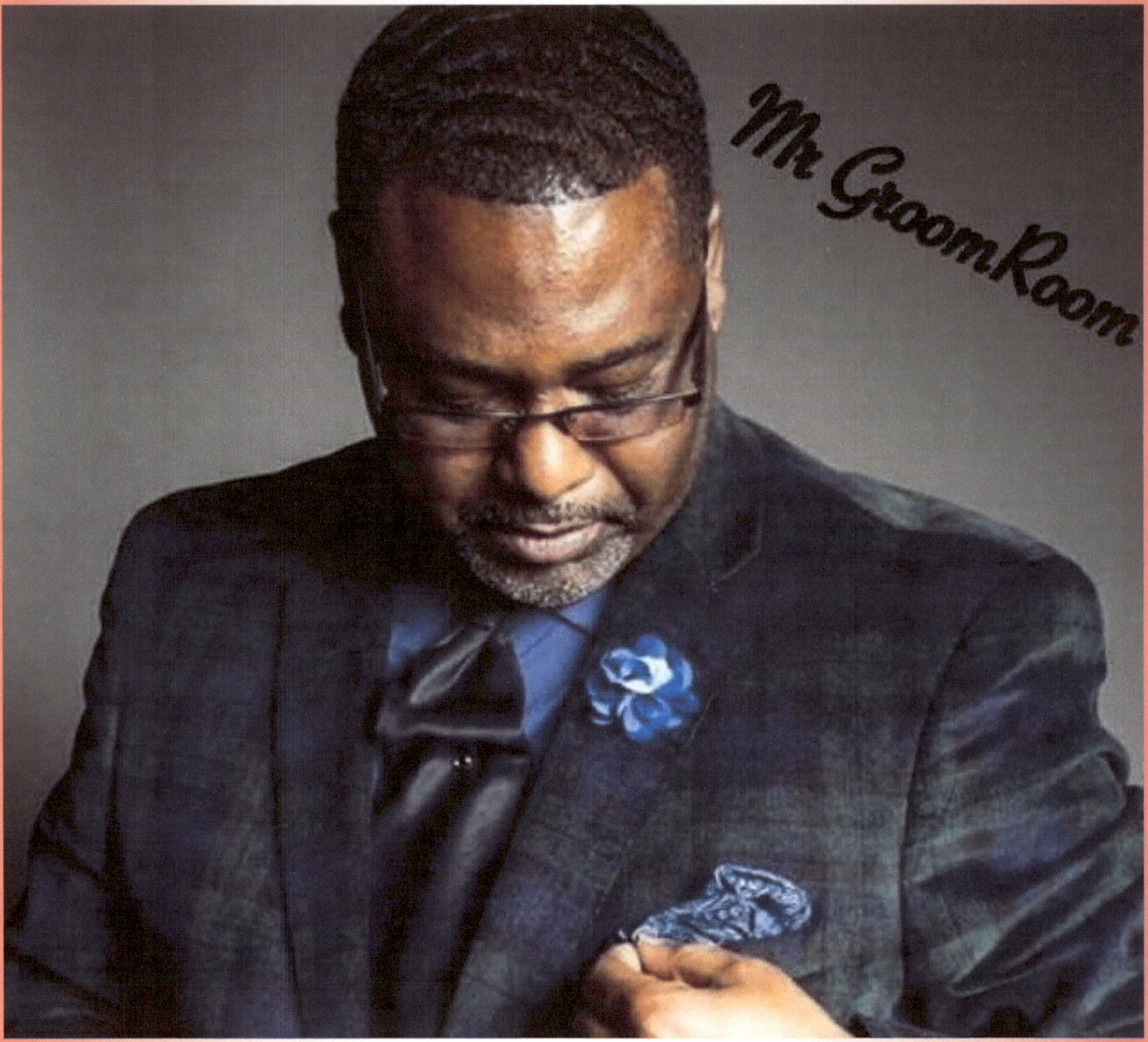

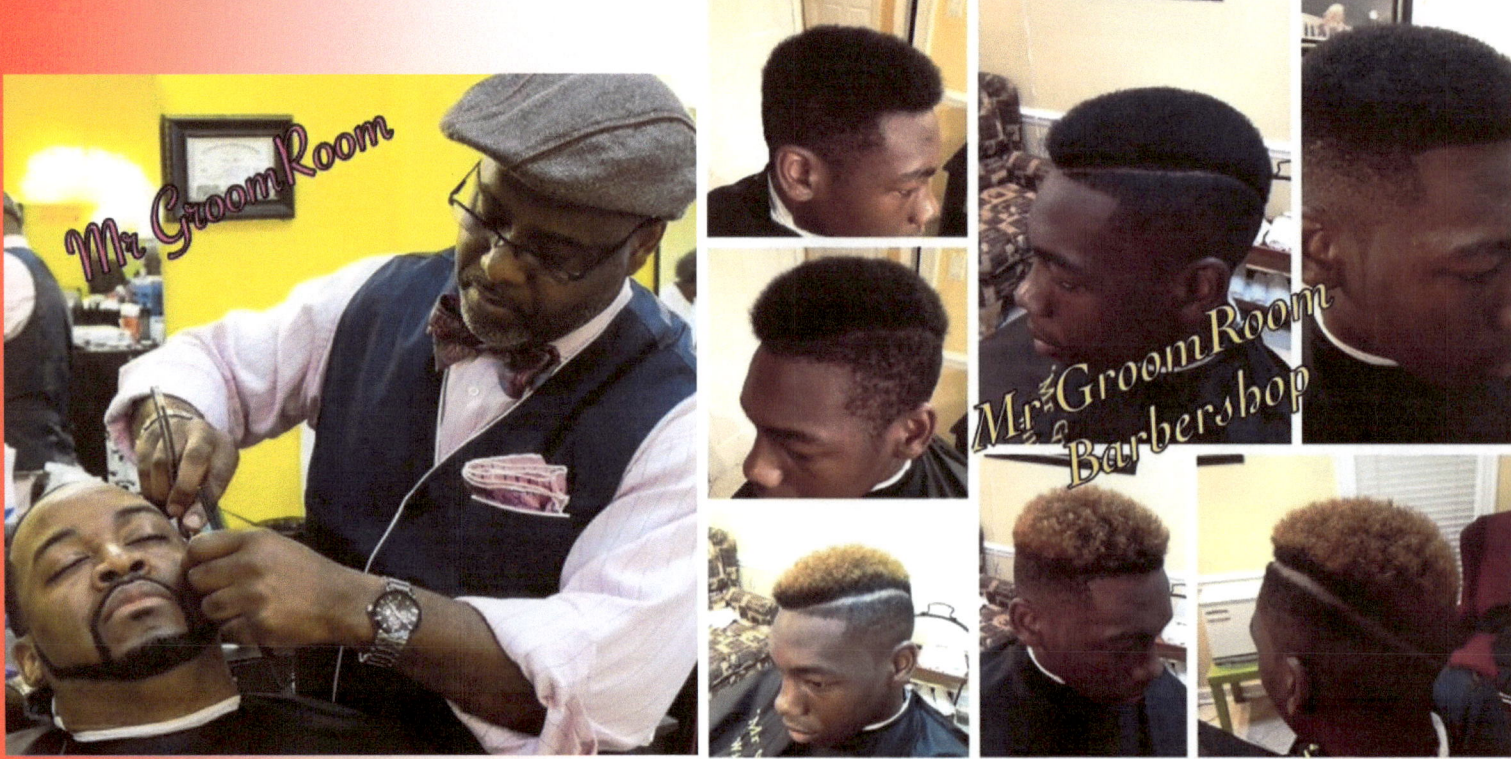

Mr GroomRoom

Mr GroomRoom

Mr GroomRoom Barbershop

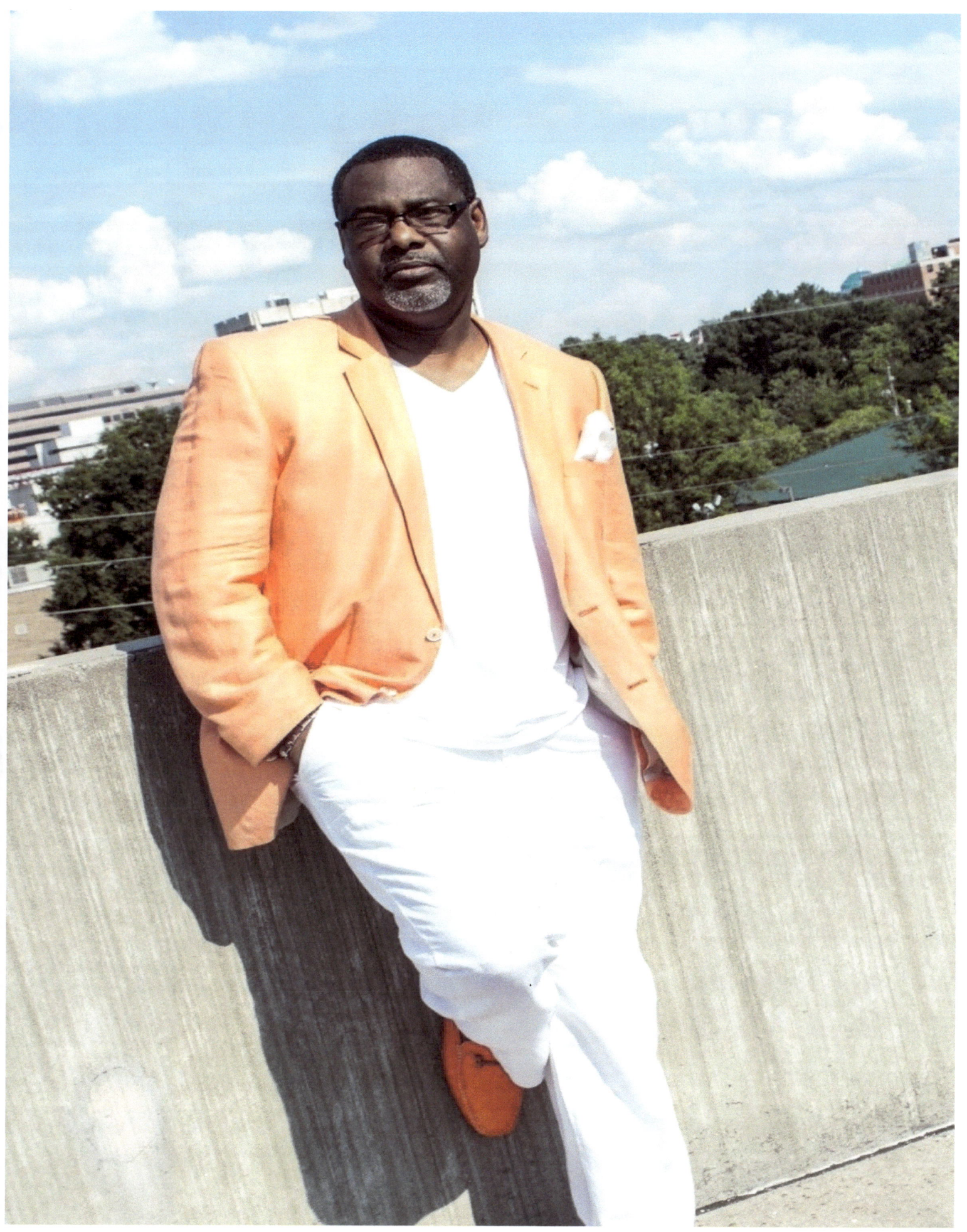

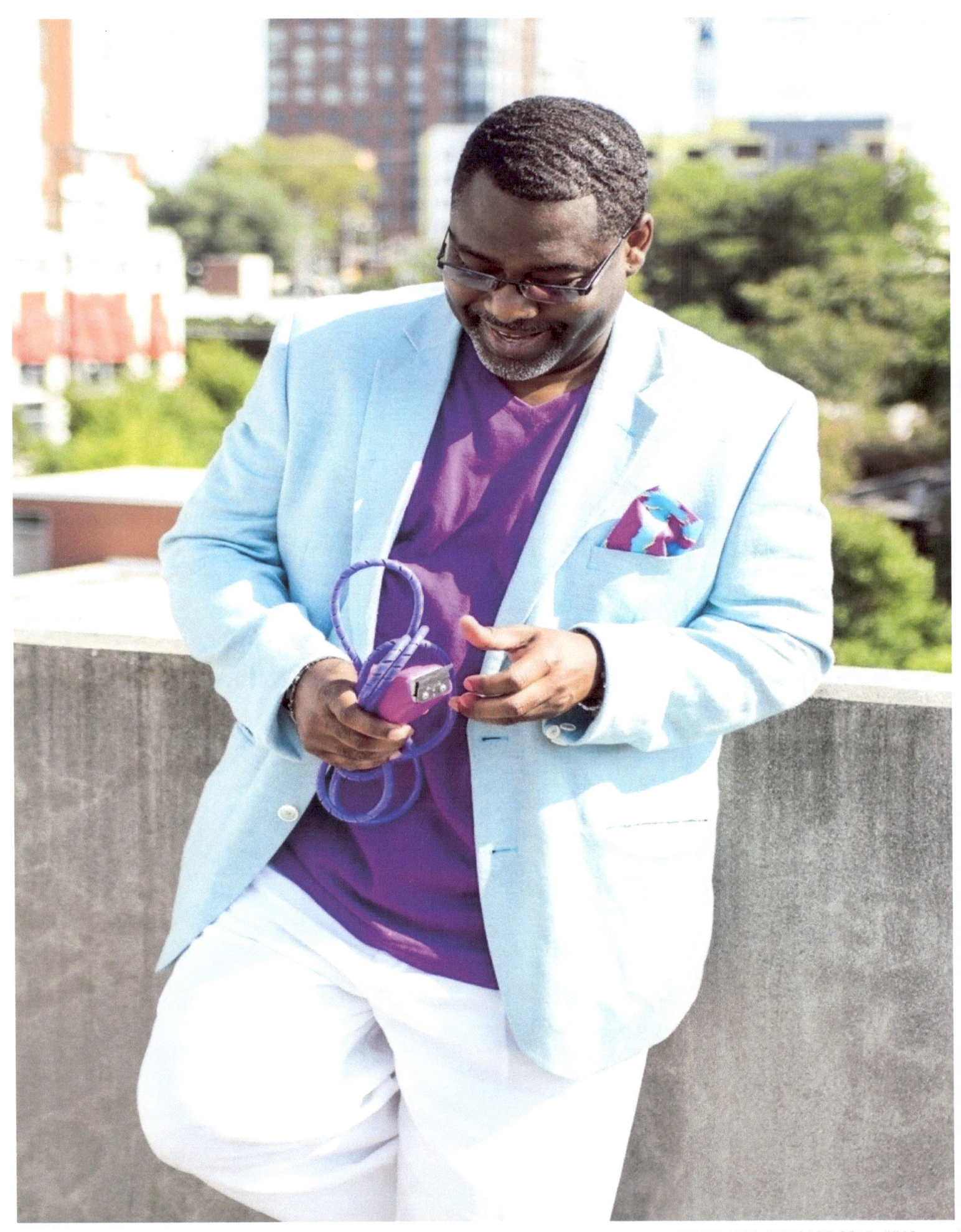

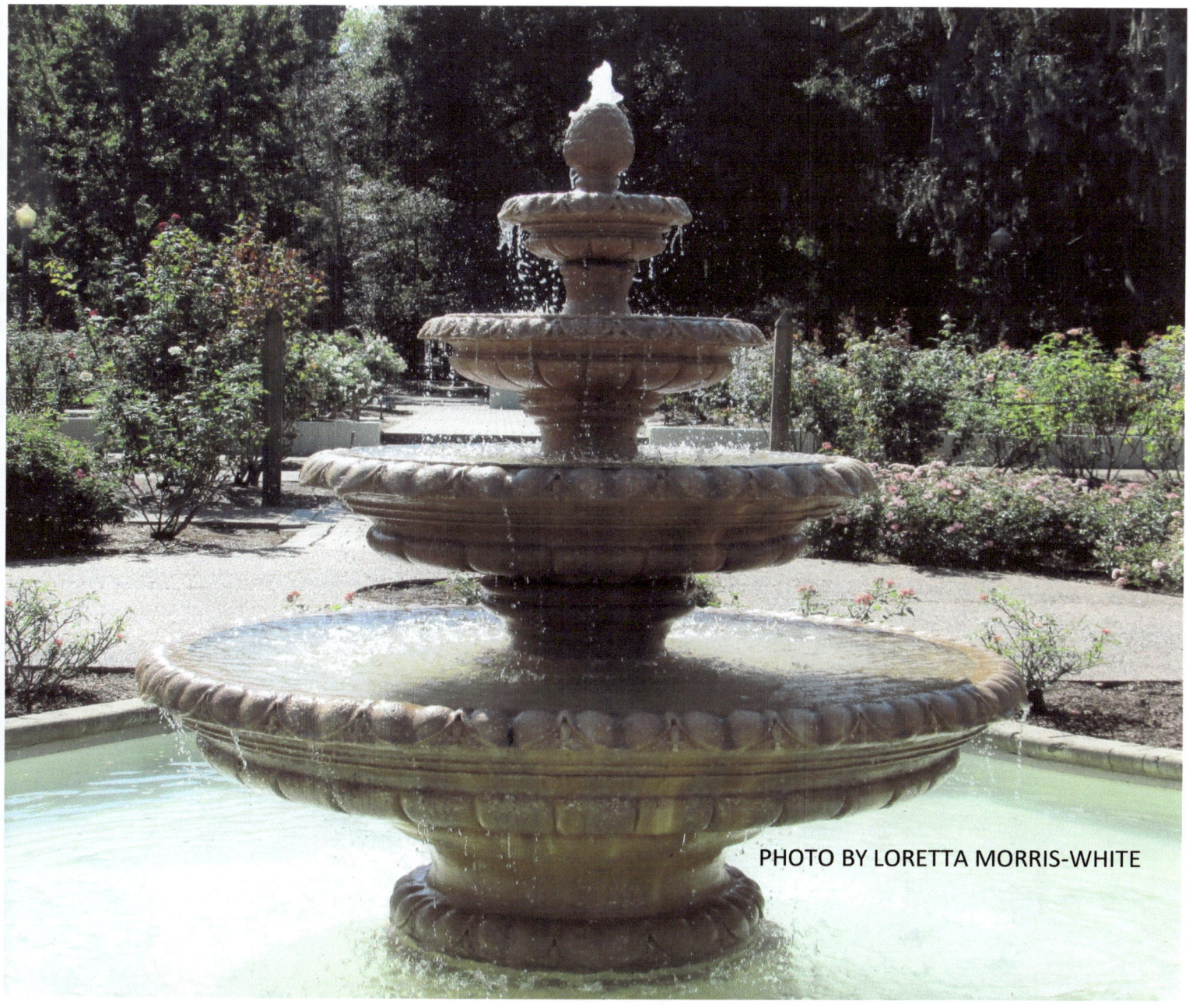

PHOTO BY LORETTA MORRIS-WHITE

PHOTOGRAPHY, WHAT AN AWESOME WAY TO CAPTURE THE BEAUTY OF NATURE.

LORETTA FOUND THE BEAUTY OF NATURE WHILE SERVING IN THE MILITARY. SHE TRAVELED AROUND THE WORLD AND DISCOVERED THE BEAUTY OF COLORADO SPRINGS, COLORADO. THAT TOPPED IT OFF. AFTER HER TIME SERVED IN THE MILITARY, SHE ENROLLED IN COLLEGE. HER CURRICULM INCLUDED PHOTOGRAPHY. WHAT A DIFFERENCE IN JUST TAKING PICTURES AND BEING A PROFESSIONAL PHOTOGRAPHER

. "I EXPERIENCED LIFE DIFFERENTLY THROUGH THE LENS OF A CAMERA. IT'S ALSO THE LITTLE THINGS NOW, I THINK. NATURE IS SO MUCH MORE INTREGING. THE COLORS OF THE LEAVES ARE BRIGHTER, THE GRAINS OF SAND HAS MORE TEXTURE. THE DRIPS OF WATER SEEM LOUDER. THE SKY IS UNDESCRIBABLE AND THE OCEAN HAS WAVES THAT YOU COUND NOT POSSIBLY EXPLAIN IN WORDS."

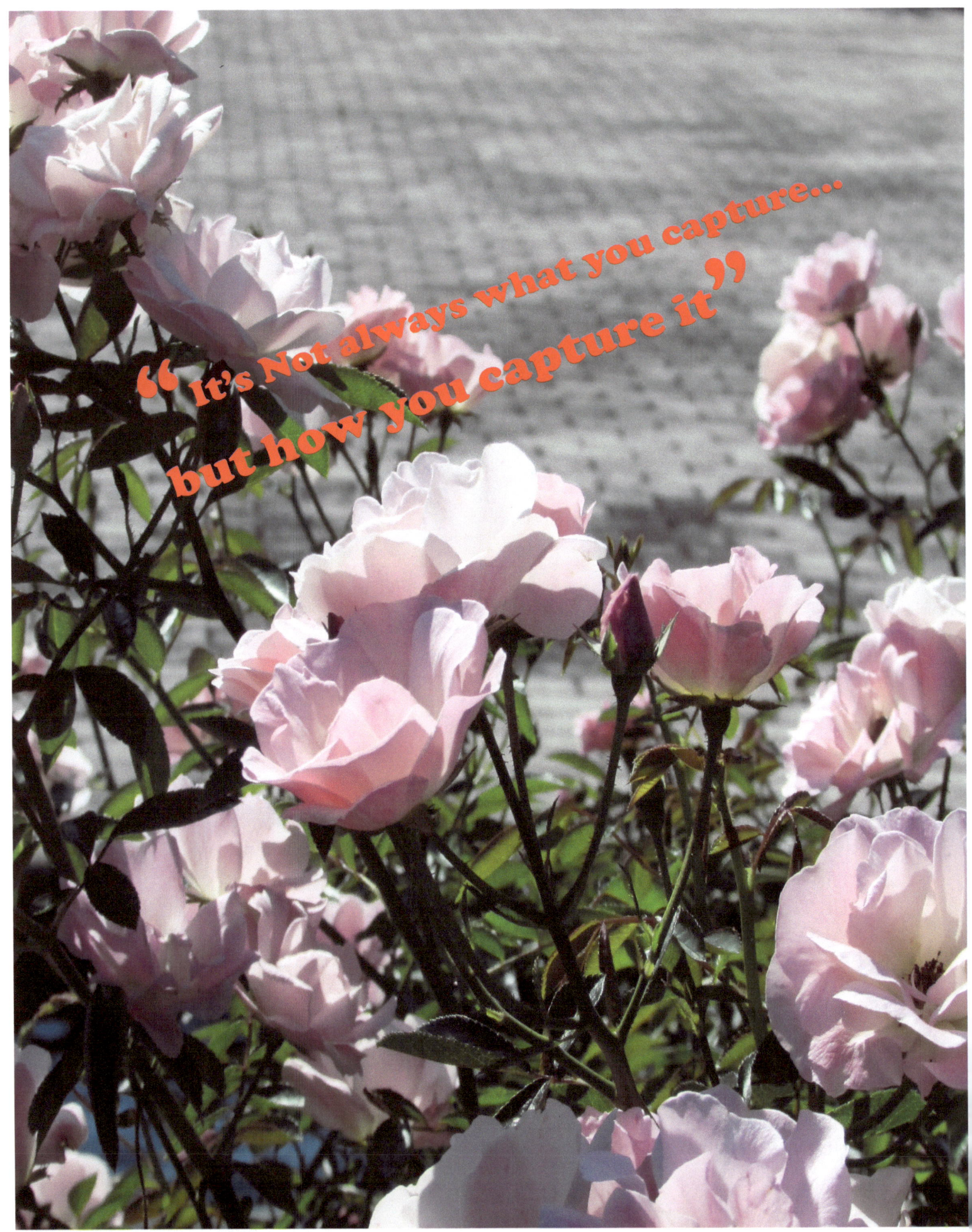

"It's Not always what you capture... but how you capture it"

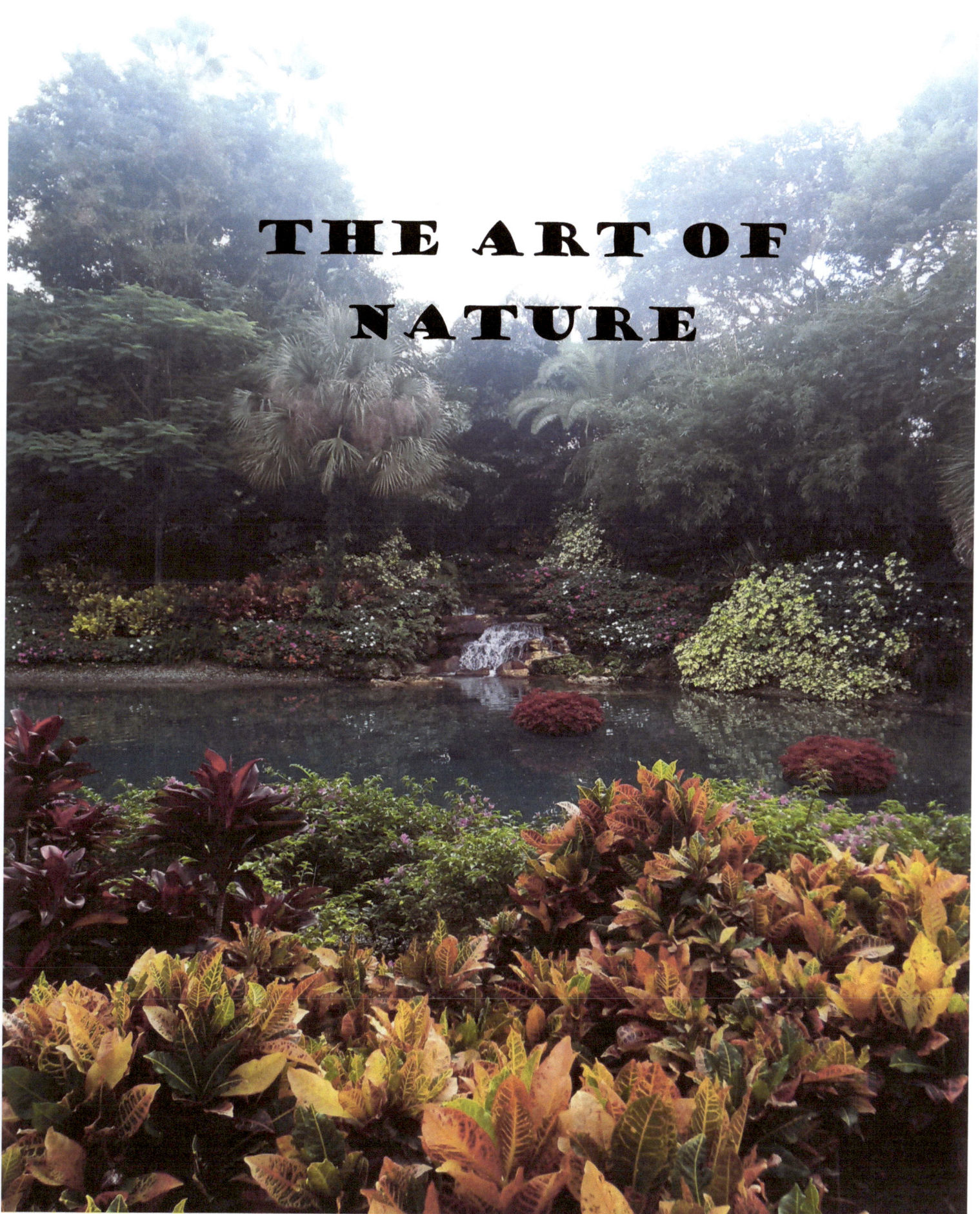

THE ART OF NATURE

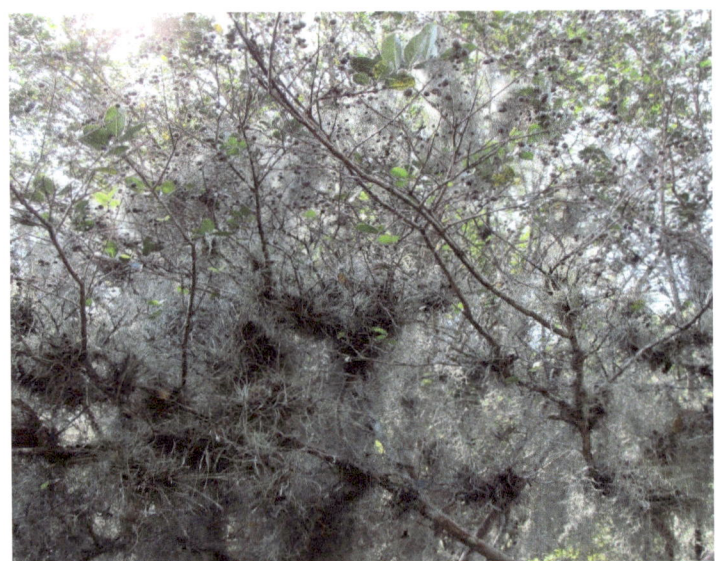

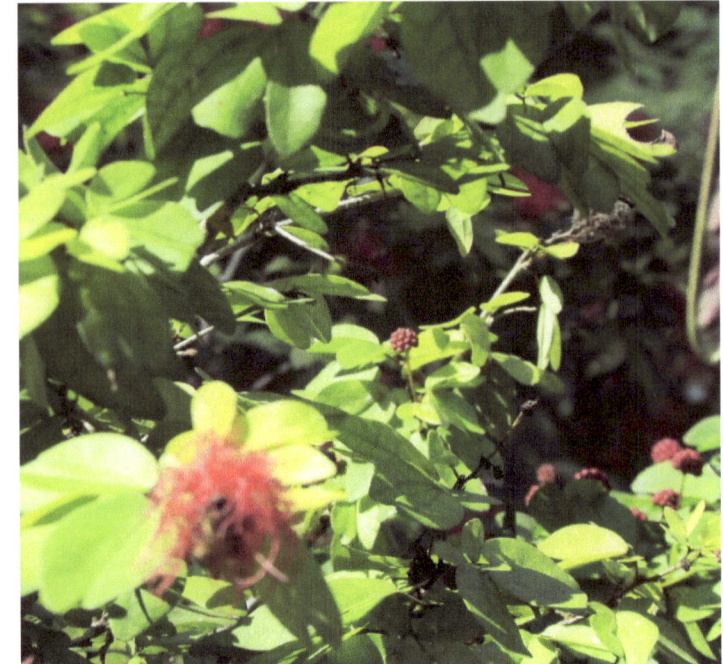

All Photos by Loretta White

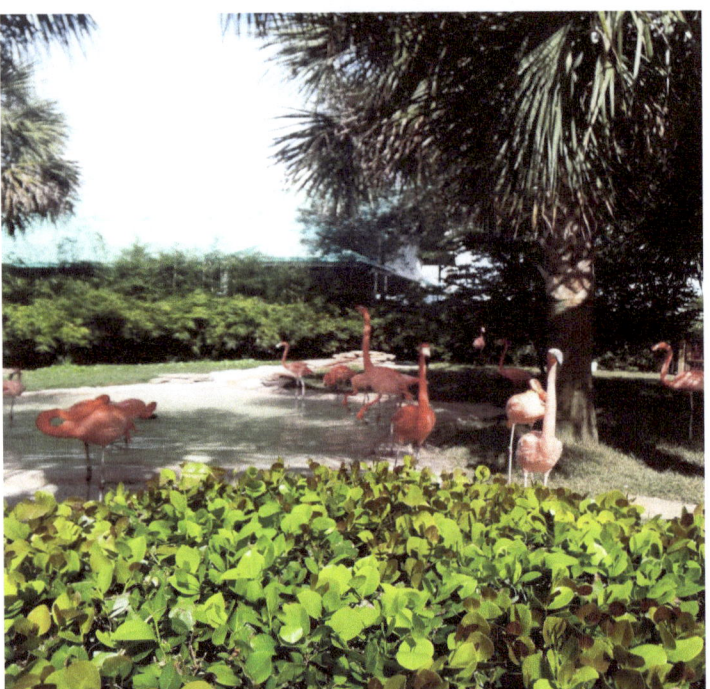

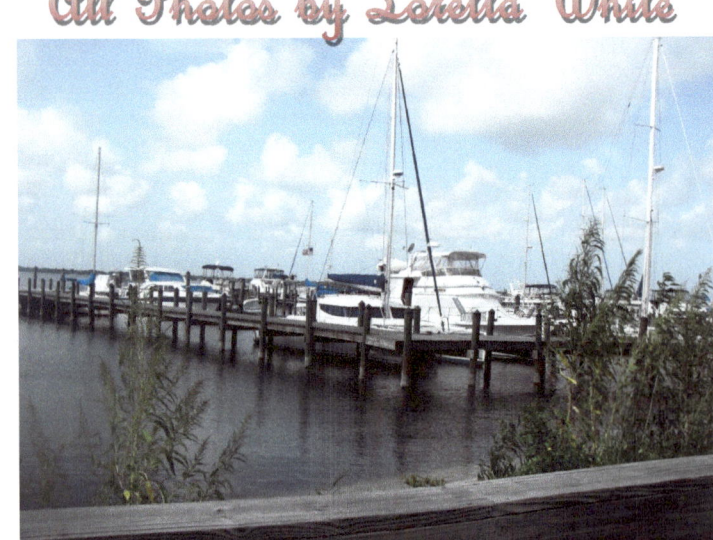

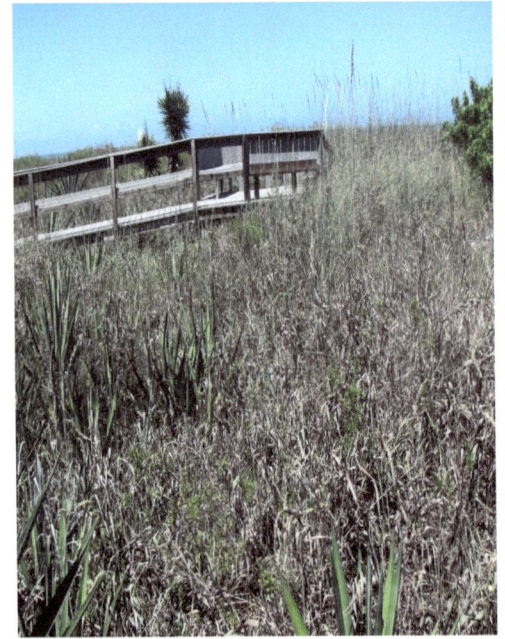

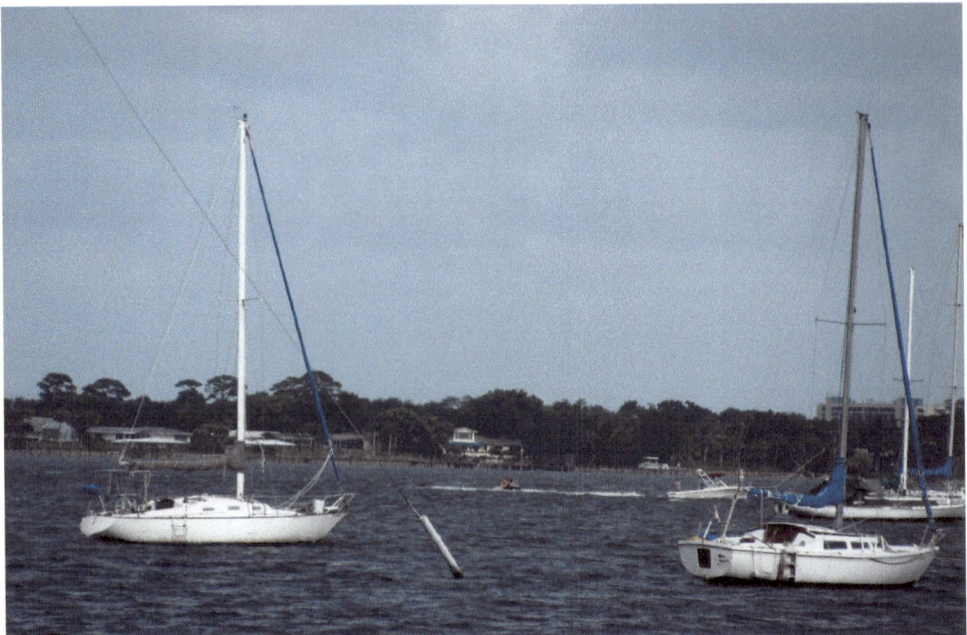

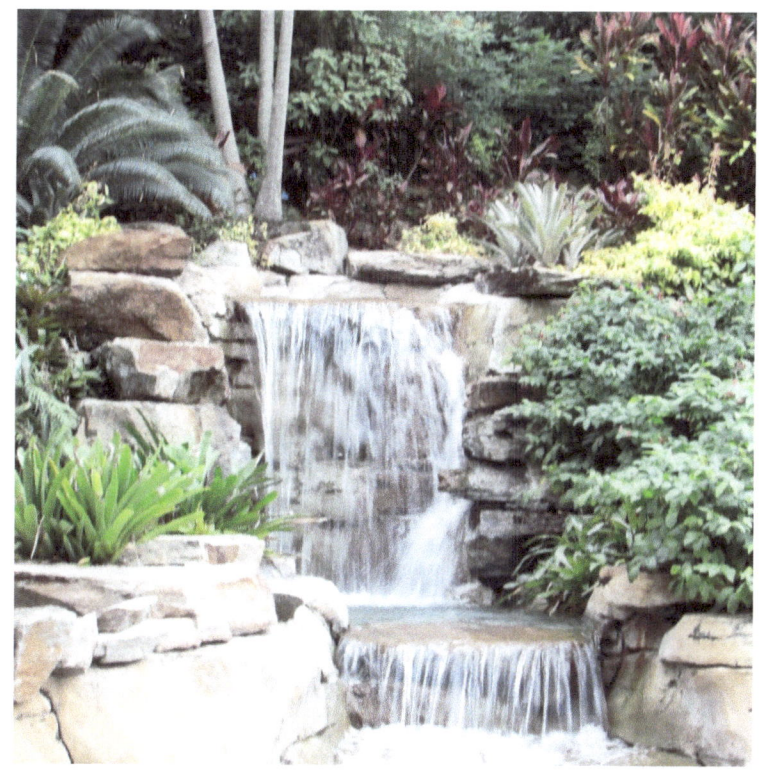

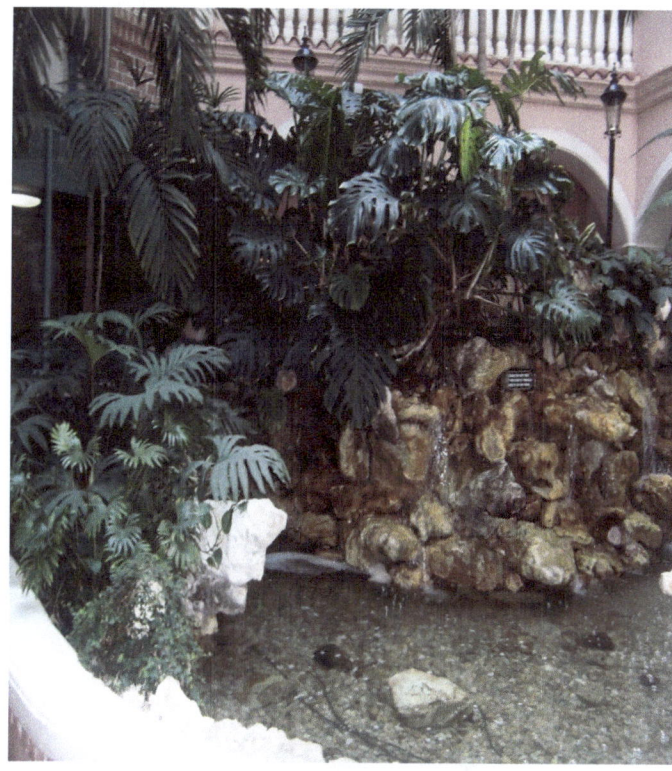

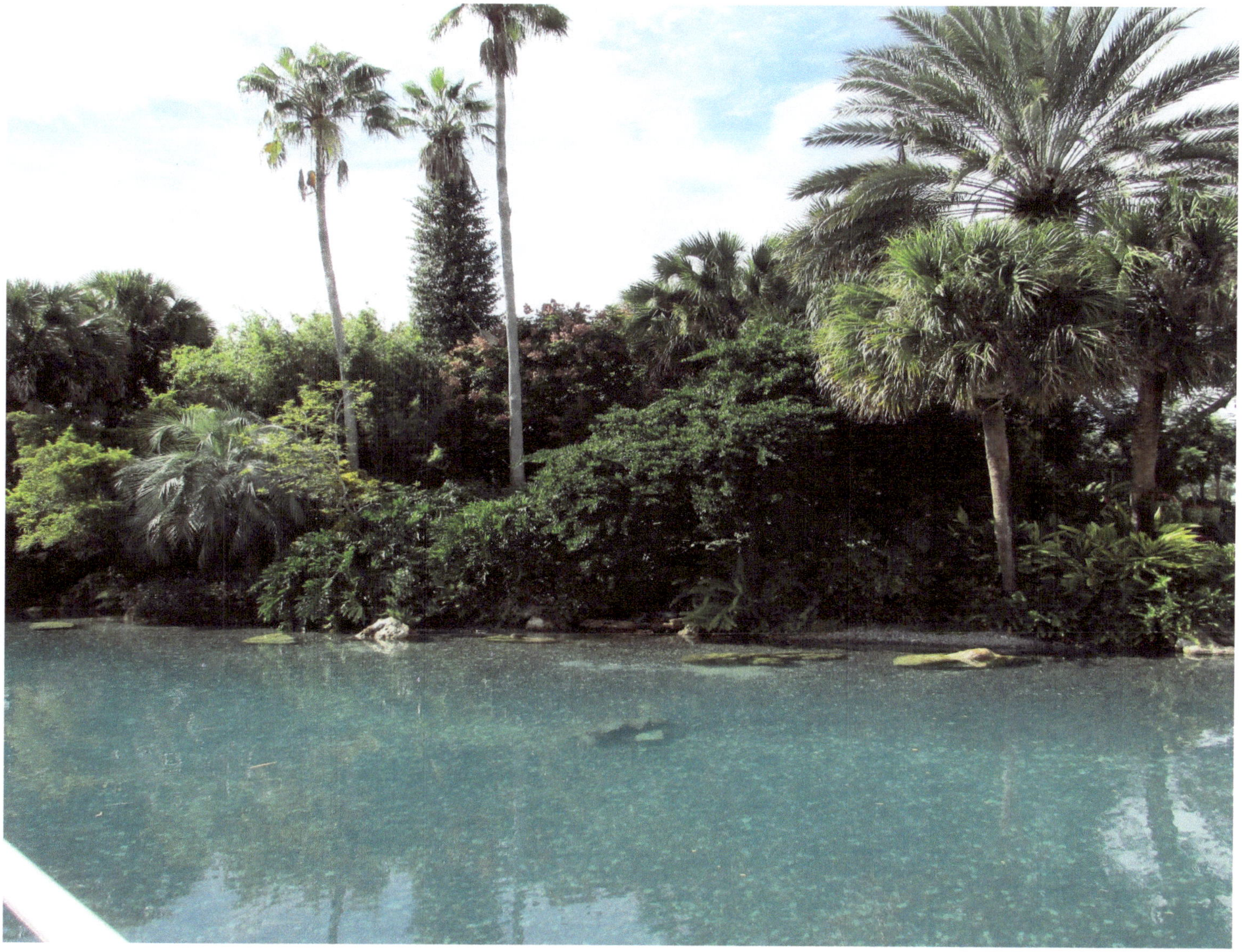

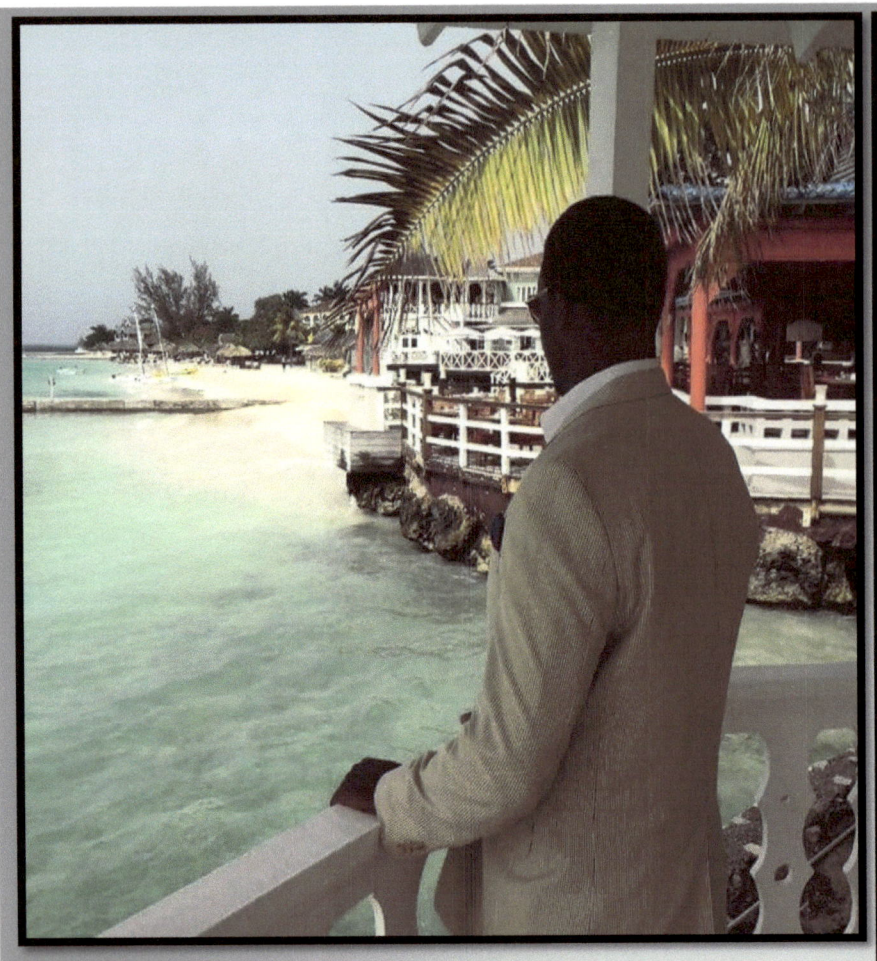

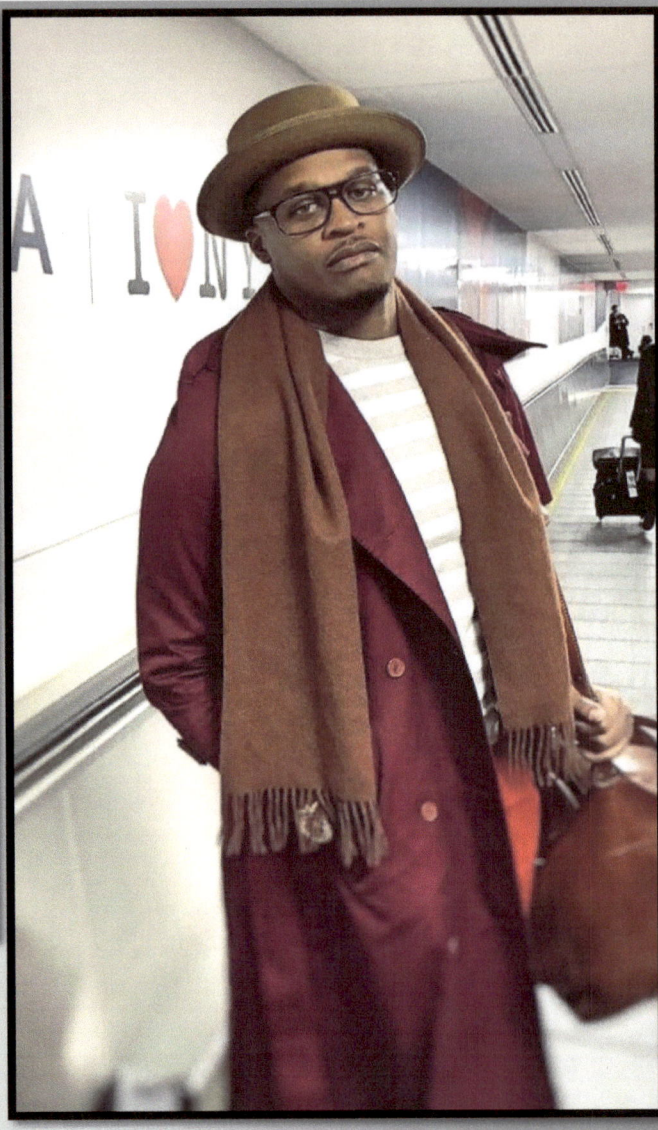

𝓜r. Kwame Lee knows how to mix business with pleasure

with his Classiness and stylish ways.

Over the years this southern gentleman has continued to refine and cultivate the overall love for the social sciences. Through ongoing observations and a heavy dose of life, Kwame has set out to positively impact the world by teaching people how to self-regulate prior to conflict. One of his primary focuses is to highlight the importance of balance, serenity and relationship in our everyday lives. Kwame is the youngest of his 3 siblings. He settled in the Tidewater area of Virginia after humble beginnings in Brook-lyn, NY. Kwame earned a Bachelor's of Science at Public Administration before going to receive a Master of Education at Cambridge College. This young man continues to work in the human services field as he seeks to give the youth that he serves the tools necessary to become productive citizens. Kwame is currently working to open his very own private foster care agency and is also finalizing a company that specializes in mediation and other family services. Kwame has dedicated his life to ensuring that people worldwide understand the importance of the human spirit and how our connectedness impacts our overall health. This single father of four is at the best when cultivating his passions and making a positive impact in the lives of others.

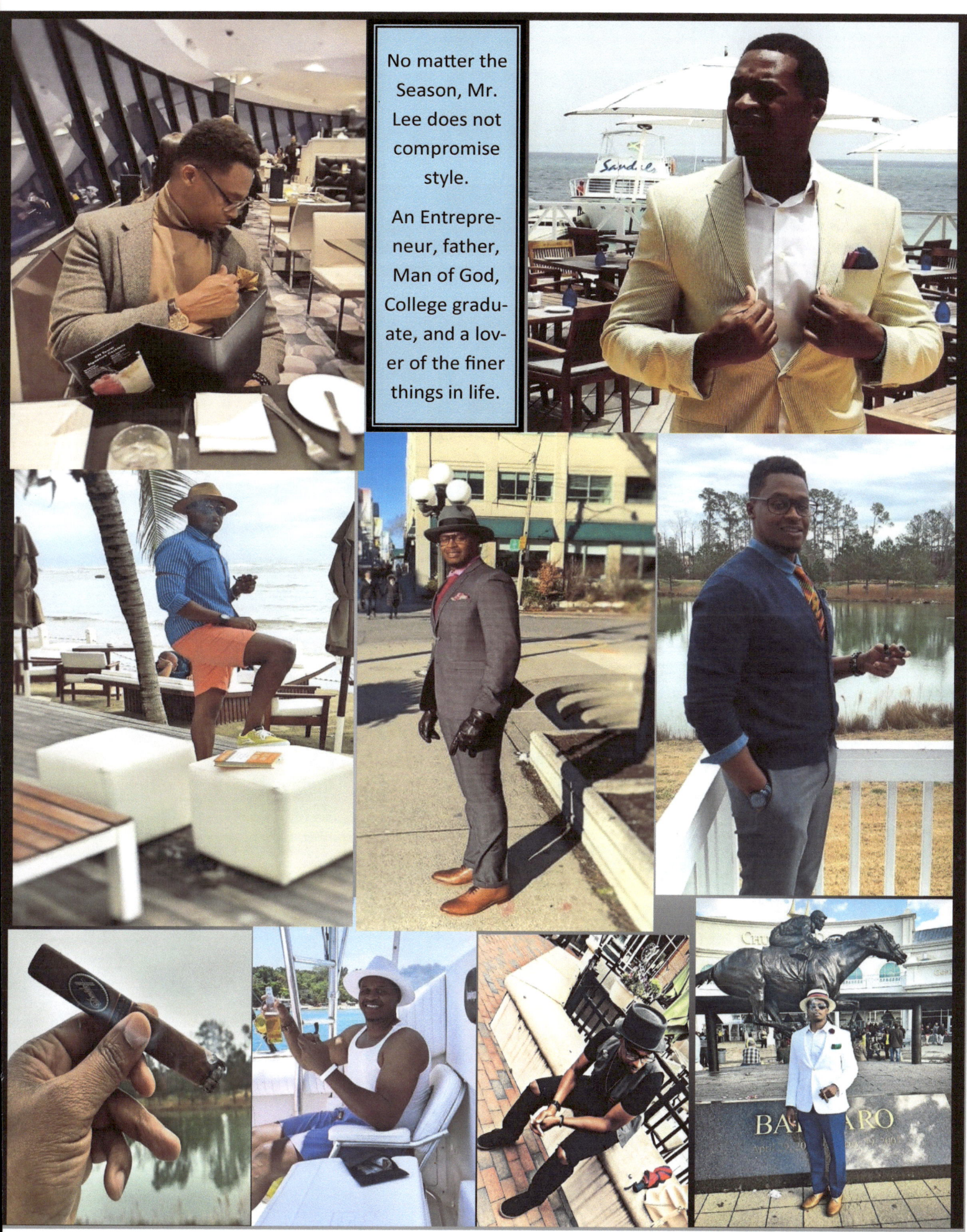

No matter the Season, Mr. Lee does not compromise style.

An Entrepreneur, father, Man of God, College graduate, and a lover of the finer things in life.

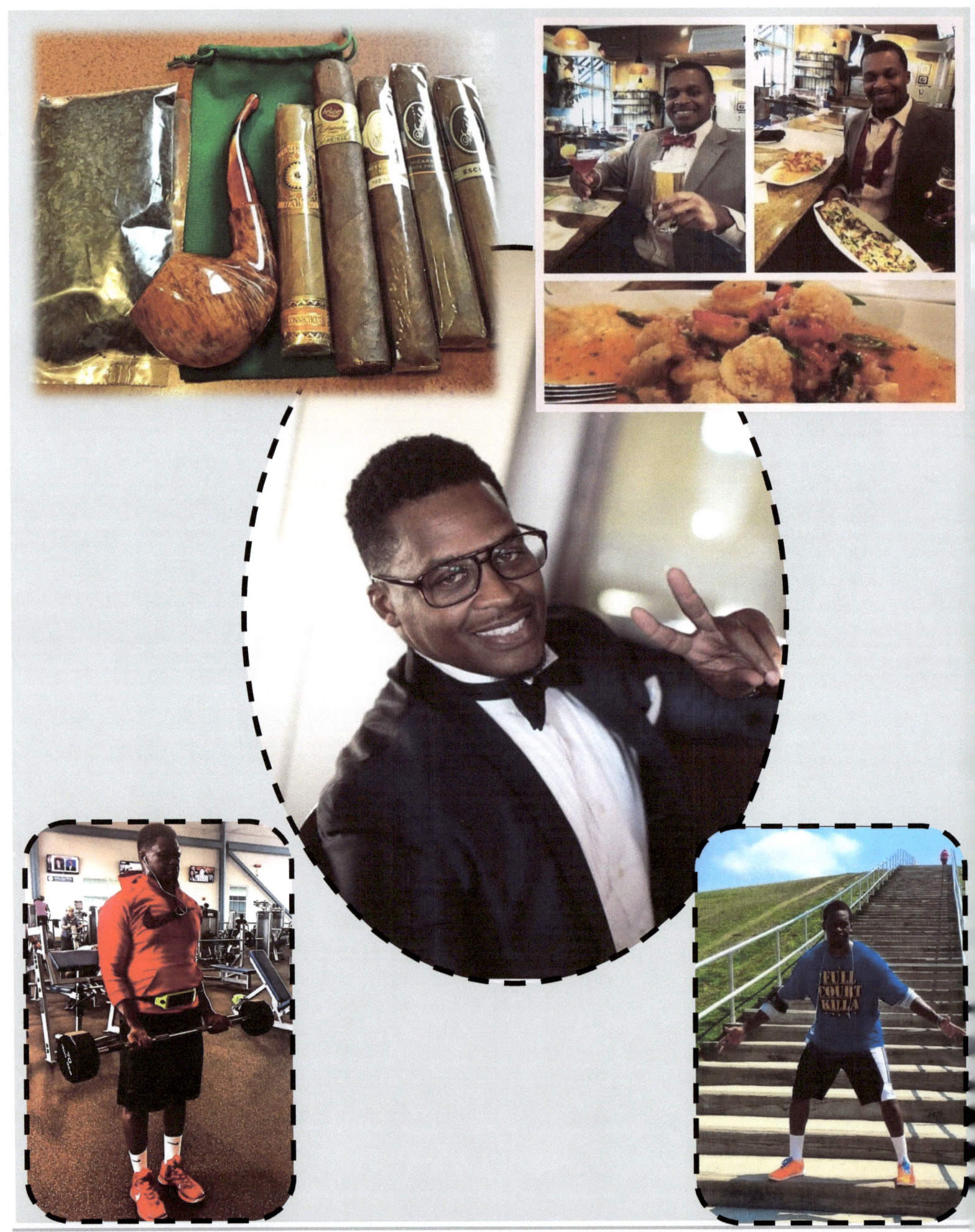

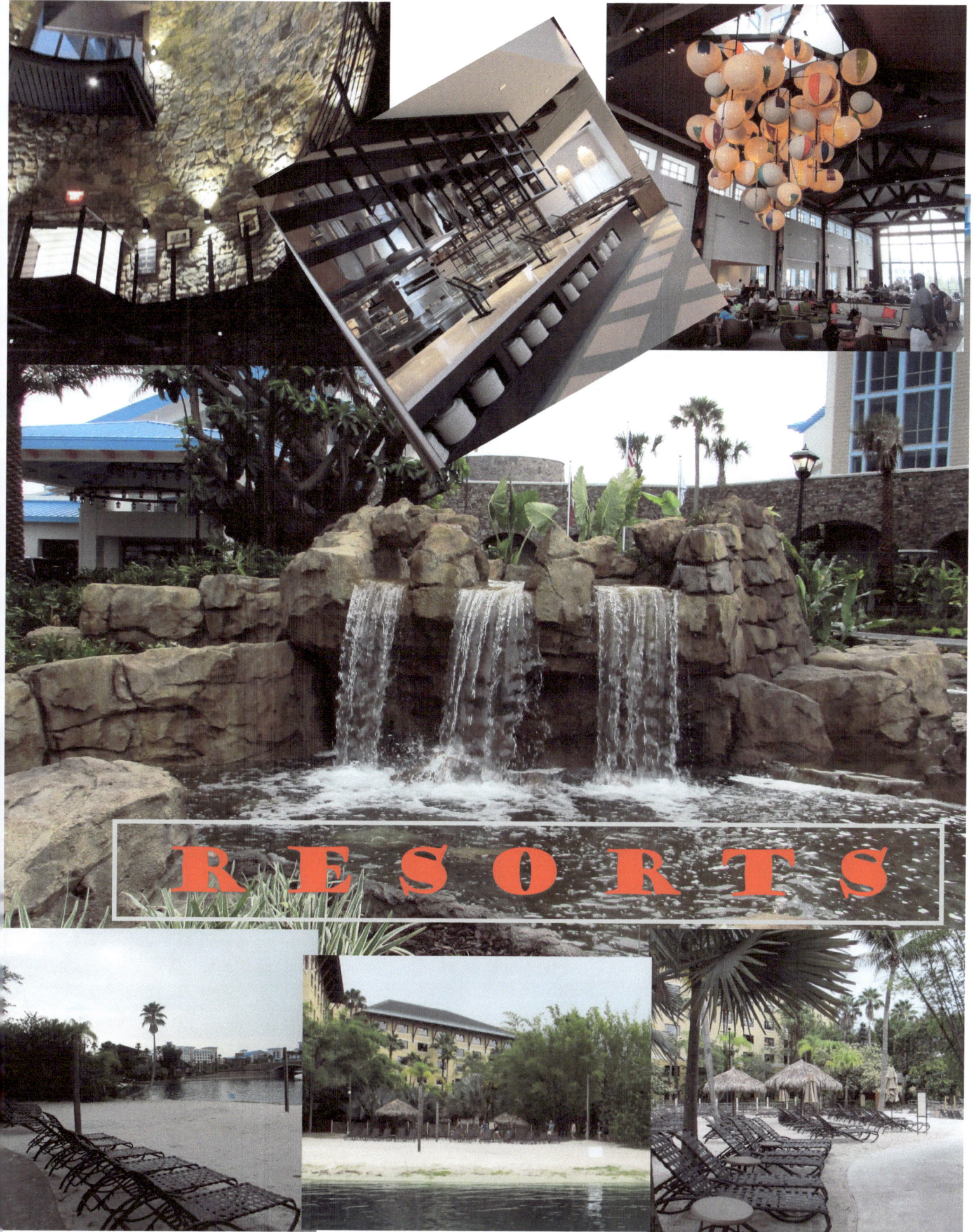

RESORTS

COZEE CAFE

WWW.COZEECAFE.COM

1145 TOWNPARK AVE.

LAKE MARY, FL. 32746

(407)804-0066

They are on FACEBOOK!

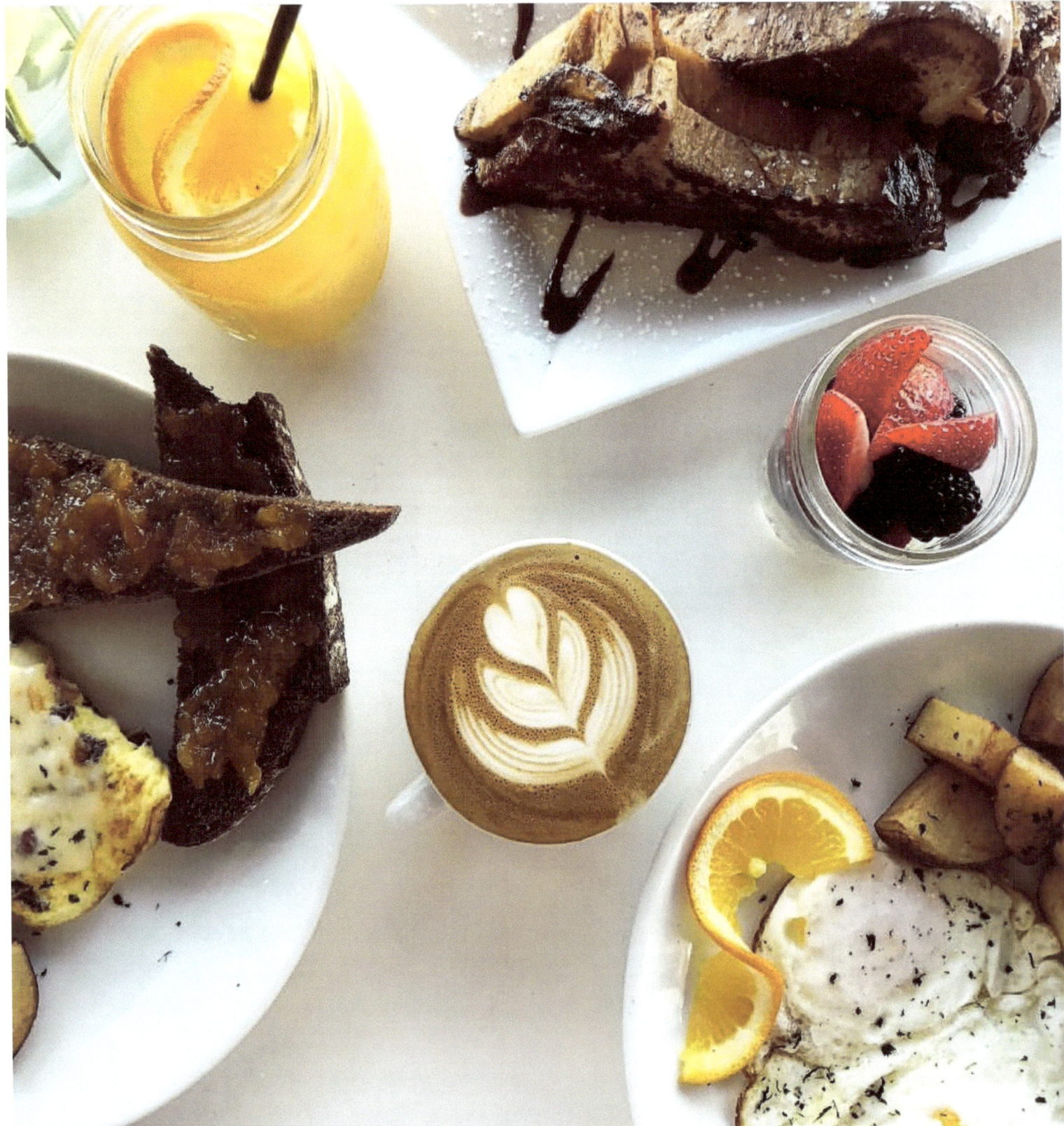

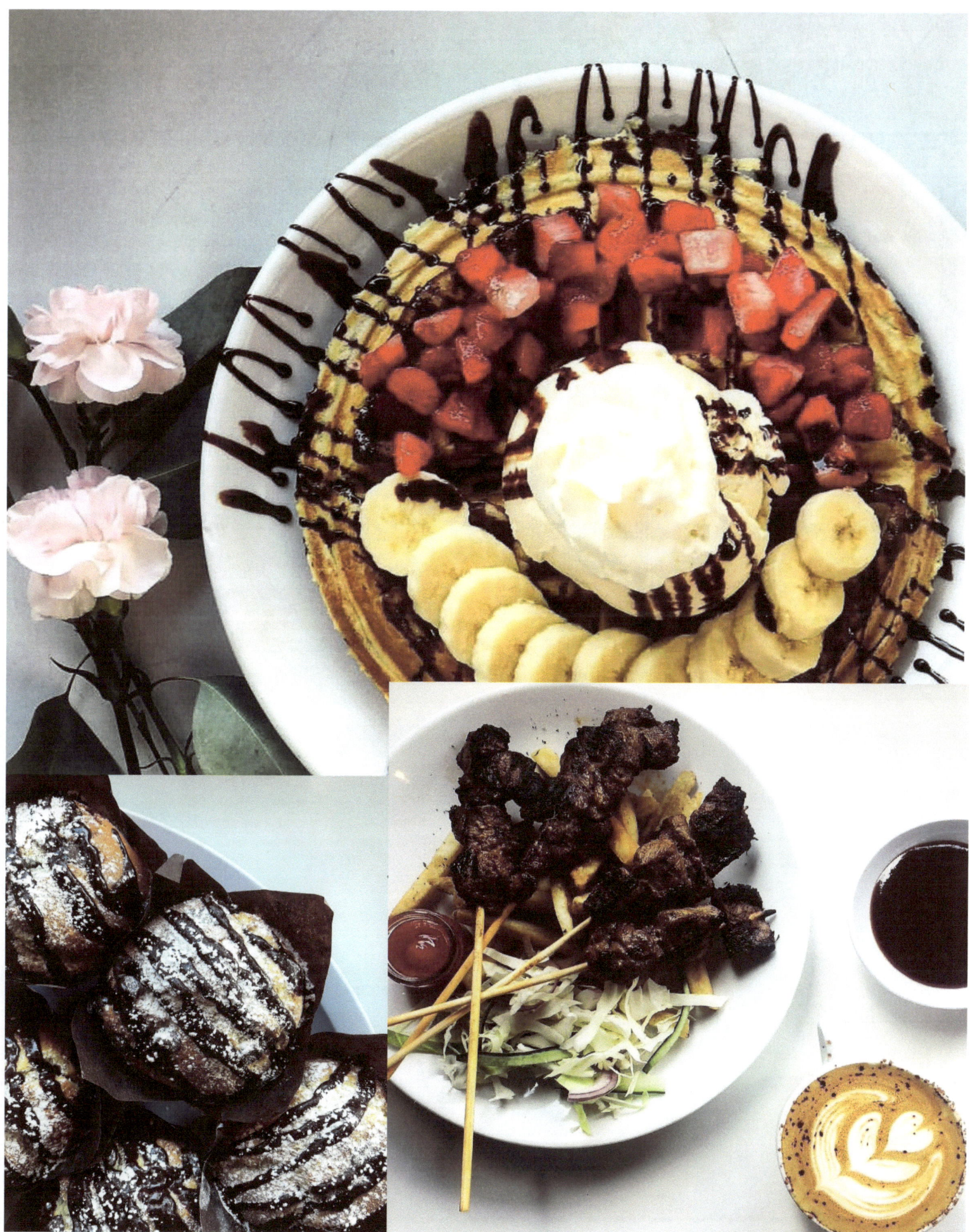

put that phone down...its family time

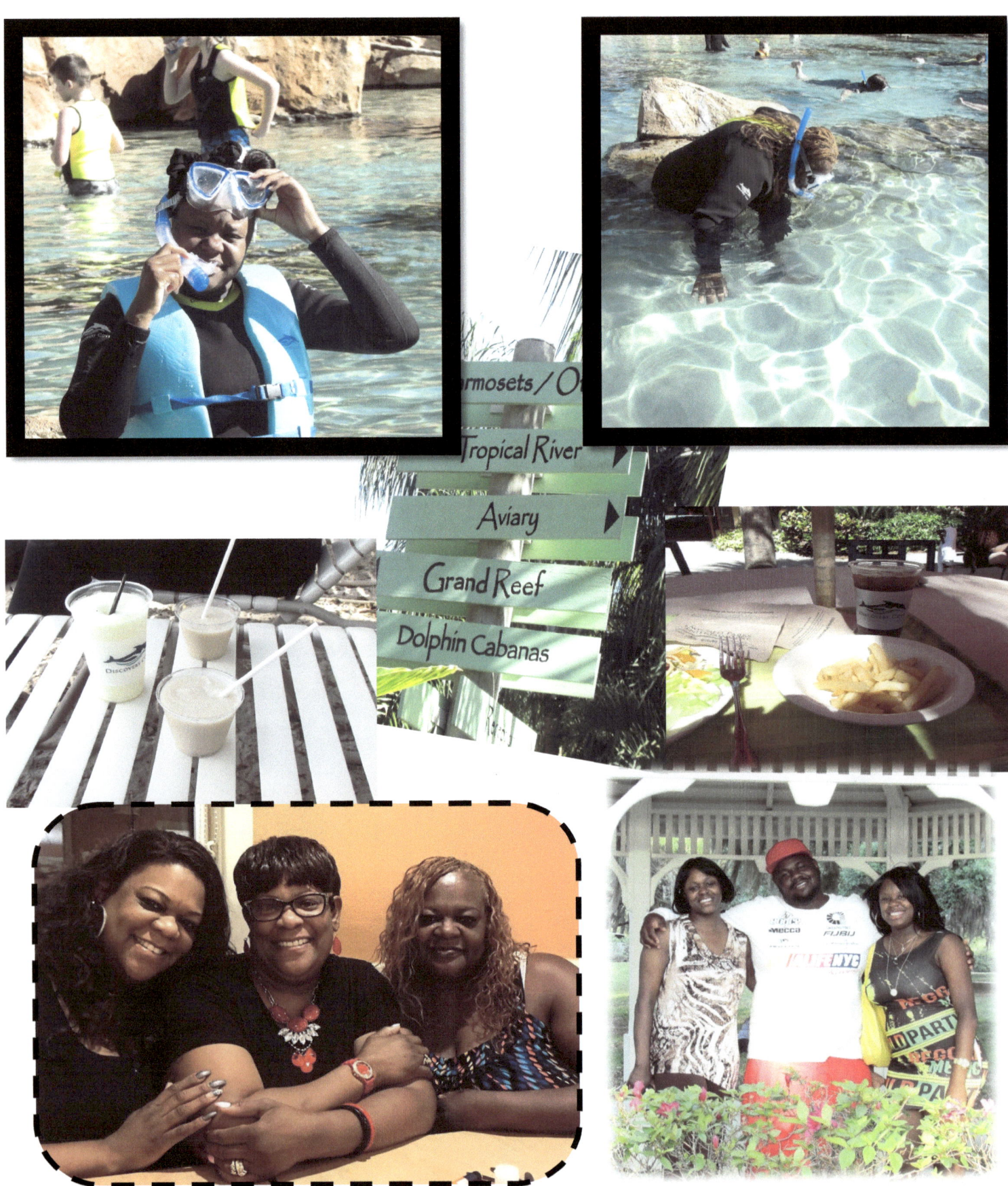

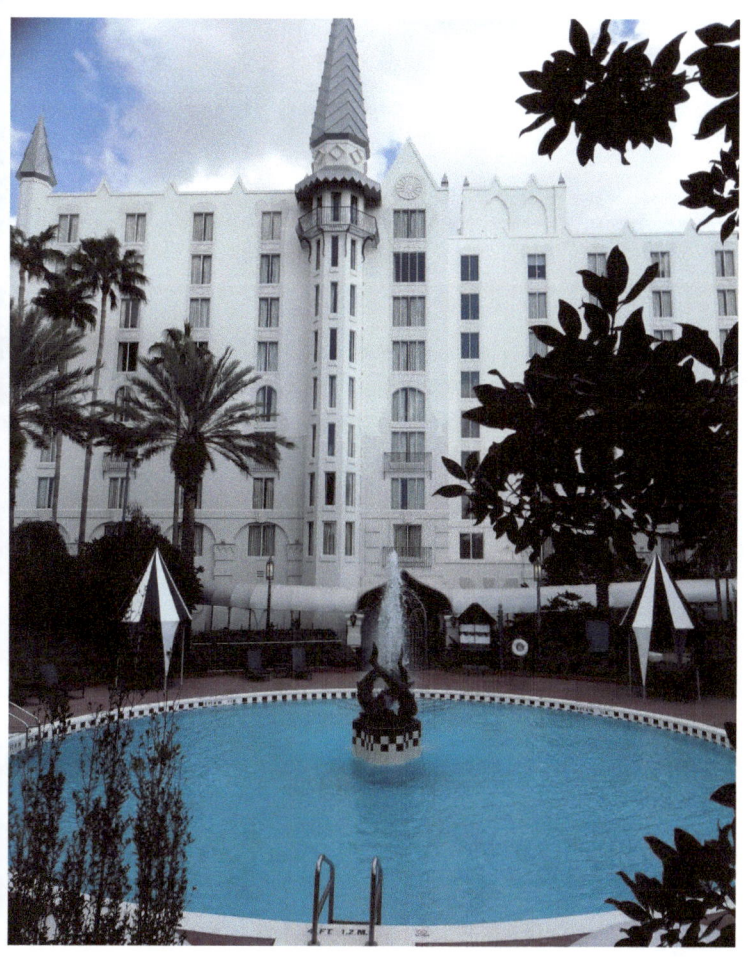

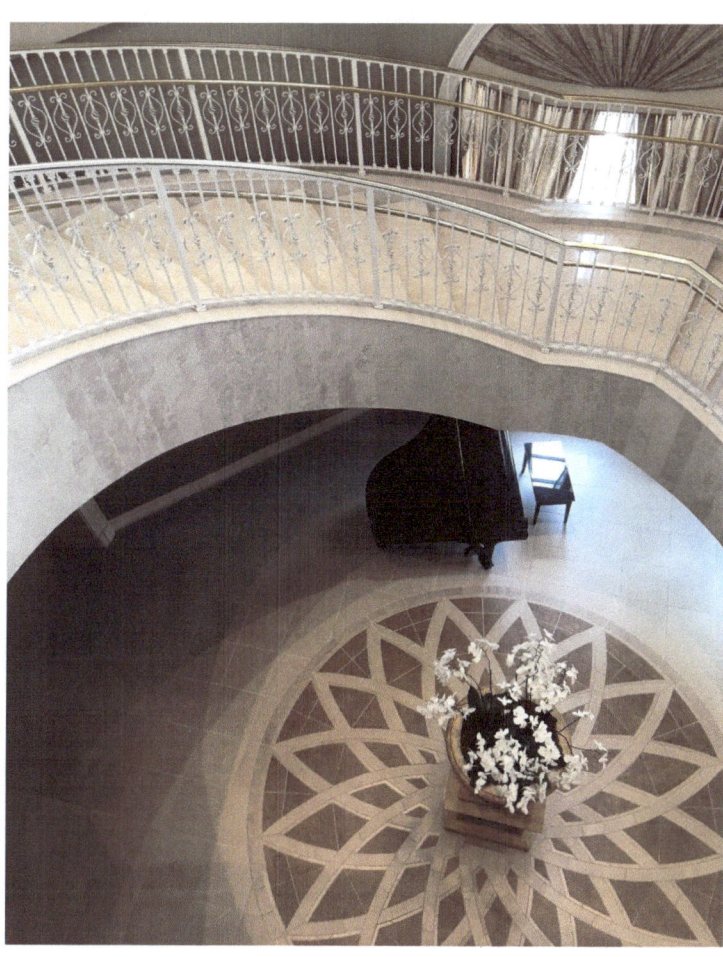

All pictures taken by Loretta Morris White

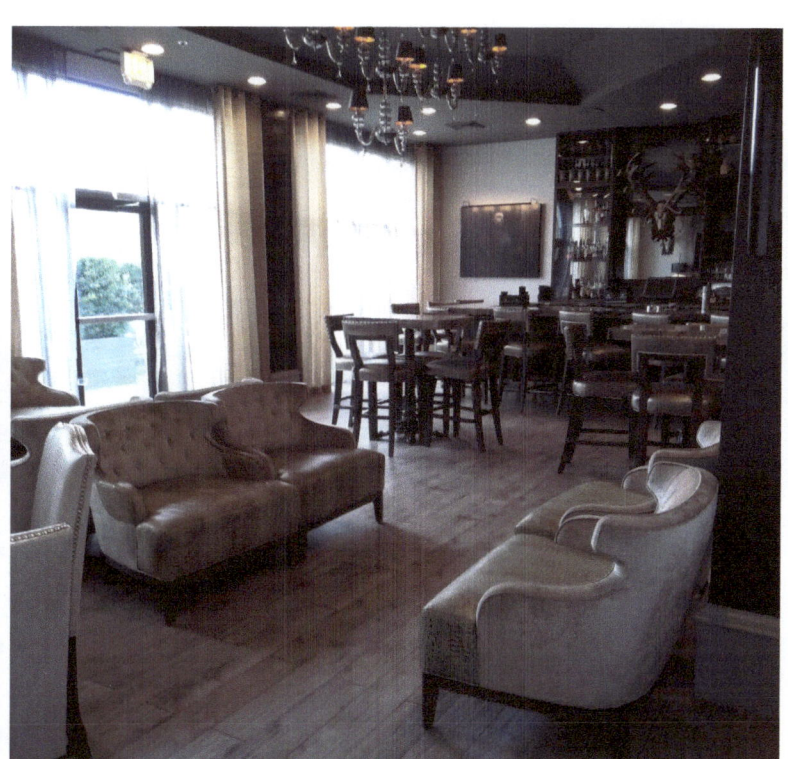

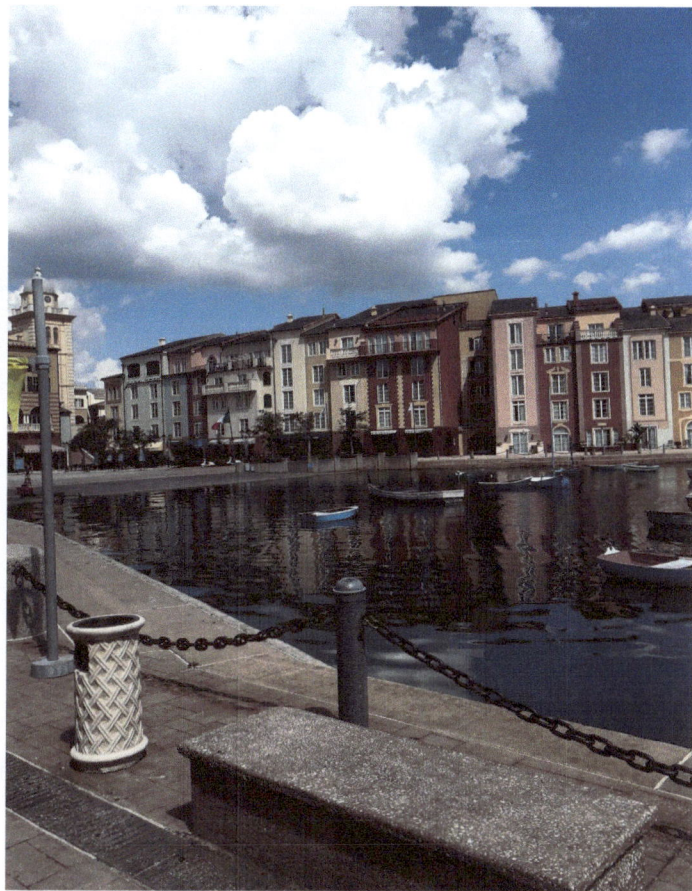

the Writers Block

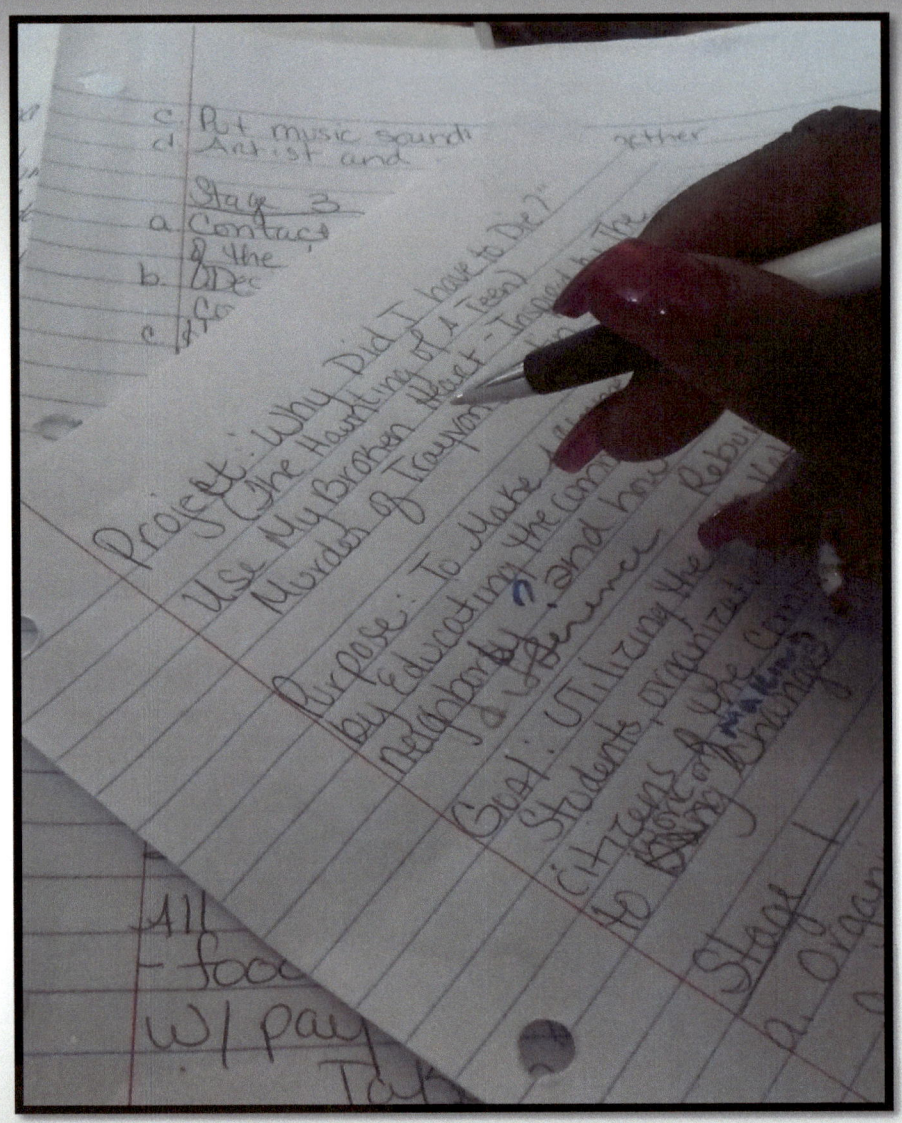

W RITERS OF ALL TYPES ARE INVITED TO JOIN US HERE. WE WANT TO SHARE NEWS, EVENTS, TALENT AND NETWORK.

BEYOND THESE NEXT FEW PAGES YOU WILL FIND GREAT AUTHORS.   PLEASE FOLLOW OUR MANY AUTHORS.

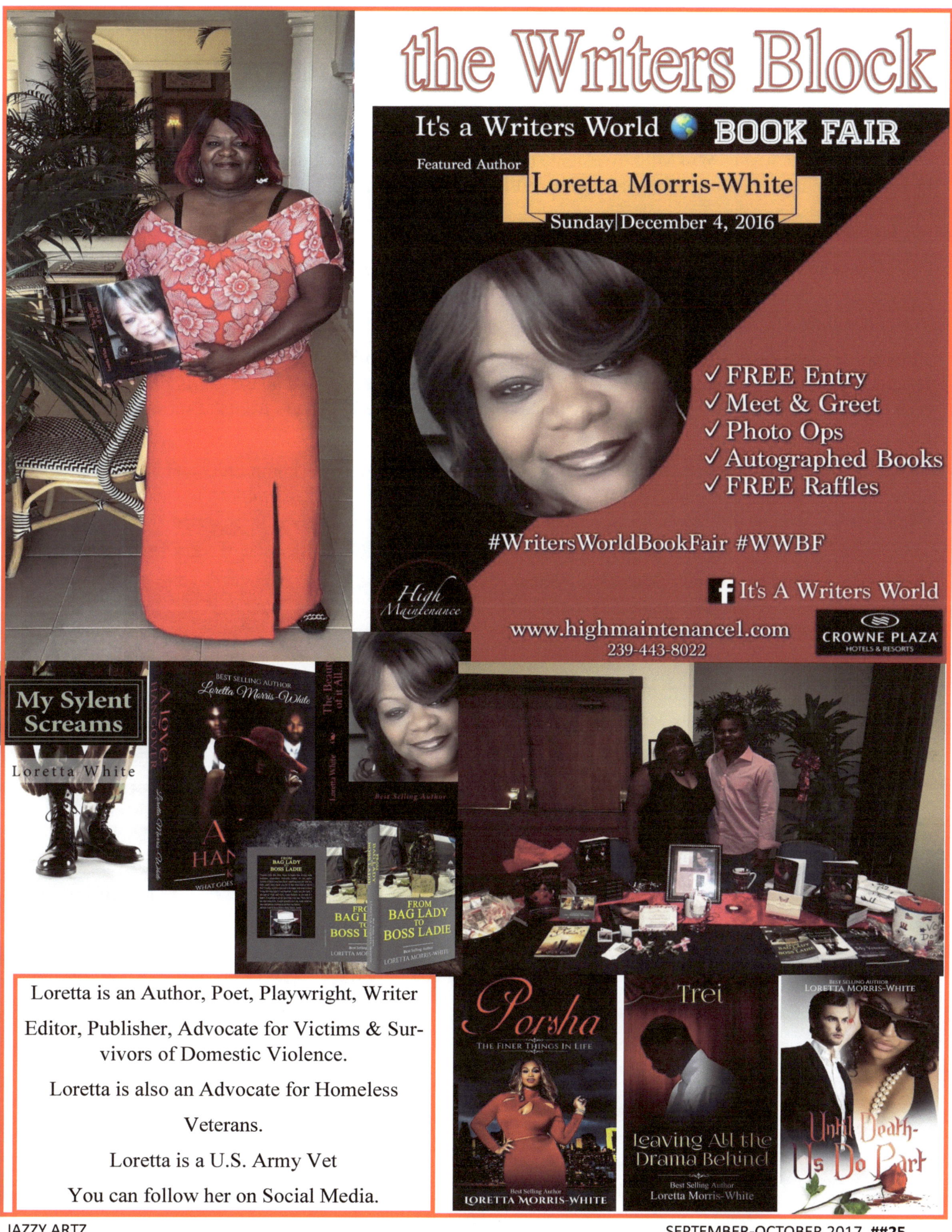

the Writers Block

It's a Writers World 🌍 BOOK FAIR

Featured Author

Loretta Morris-White

Sunday | December 4, 2016

✓ FREE Entry
✓ Meet & Greet
✓ Photo Ops
✓ Autographed Books
✓ FREE Raffles

#WritersWorldBookFair #WWBF

High Maintenance

f It's A Writers World

www.highmaintenance1.com
239-443-8022

CROWNE PLAZA
HOTELS & RESORTS

My Sylent Screams

Loretta White

BEST SELLING AUTHOR
Loretta Morris-White

A LOVE HANGOVER
WHAT GOES

The Beauty of it All...
Loretta White
Best Selling Author

FROM BAG LADY TO BOSS LADIE
Best Selling Author
LORETTA MORRIS-WHITE

Loretta is an Author, Poet, Playwright, Writer
Editor, Publisher, Advocate for Victims & Survivors of Domestic Violence.

Loretta is also an Advocate for Homeless

Veterans.

Loretta is a U.S. Army Vet

You can follow her on Social Media.

Porsha
THE FINER THINGS IN LIFE
Best Selling Author
LORETTA MORRIS-WHITE

Trei
Leaving All the Drama Behind
Best Selling Author
Loretta Morris-White

BEST SELLING AUTHOR
LORETTA MORRIS-WHITE
Until Death Us Do Part

WHAT'S YO MONEY MAKING PLAN?

BY CHRISTOPHER R. BOYD aka B.I.G CHRIS

Christopher Boyd was born to Military parents in 1990 in Raleigh, N.C. the birthplace of his mom. He has three sisters, one brother and a Nephew living in Florida. He was raised in Florida, therefore, this is where he calls home.

Chris experienced trauma early in his life and searched for an outlet. Sports was his first choice because that's what he was introduced to in his neighborhood as he grew. He would go to the basketball court everyday and then he discovered the Boys and Girls club in the same vicinity. He became a Volunteer and also starter mentoring the other young boys.

Chris was raised practically by his mom where he learned to be humble and how to trust and believe in God. He enjoyed sharing his time with others that were suffering from neglect and abuse. Chris finally started his own basketball team and they played many places and enjoyed meeting others from the surrounding communities.

Chris later found an interest in Music. His mom would mentor youth in the community and host talent shows. This is when Chris realized that it took so much commitment and hard work to be the best at something that you wanted to become successful in.

After years of practice and disappointments, Chris decided to start his very own Independent Record Production company. He also realized that it would take a great, strong and determined team to make it all come together.

So how would he do this? Well, this is when he came up with a plan. A Money Making Plan. He has

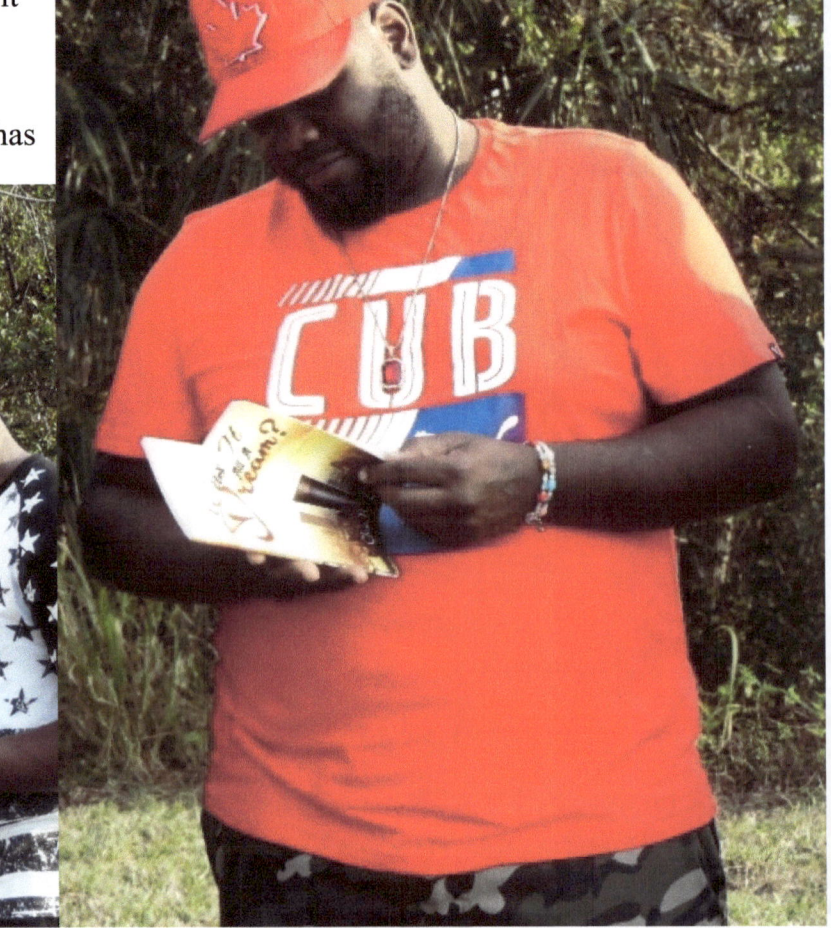

written a book with the formula to become successful at whatever it is you want to do in your life. Build your career with your very own Money Making Plan. The Book is titled, "Was It All a Dream?" You can find it on Amazon.com

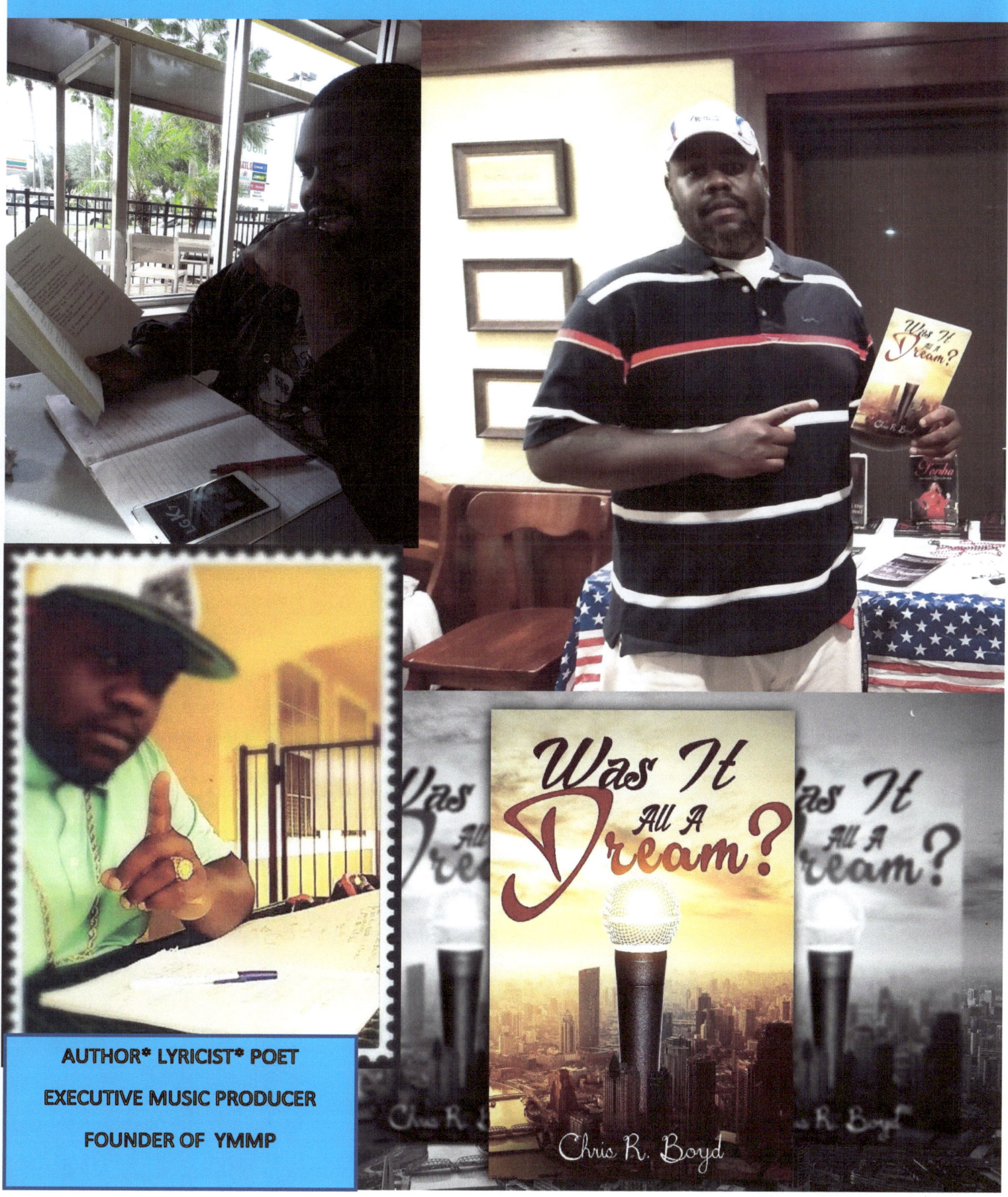

AUTHOR* LYRICIST* POET

EXECUTIVE MUSIC PRODUCER

FOUNDER OF YMMP

SP
SISTAH'S PLACE

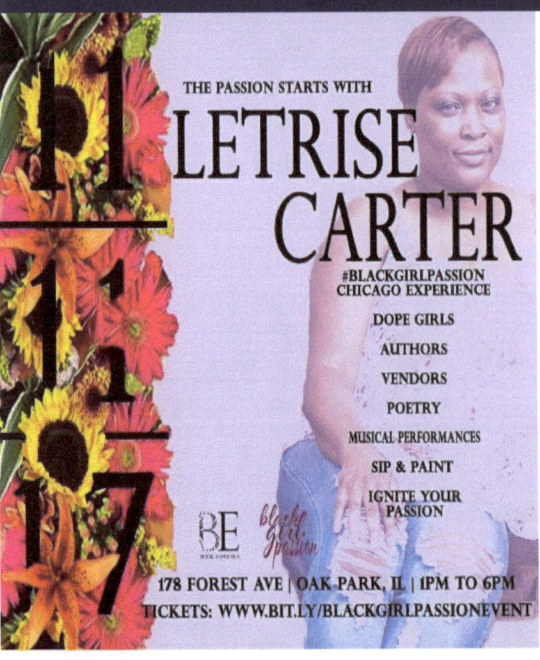

THE PASSION STARTS WITH

LETRISE CARTER

#BLACKGIRLPASSION
CHICAGO EXPERIENCE

DOPE GIRLS

AUTHORS

VENDORS

POETRY

MUSICAL PERFORMANCES

SIP & PAINT

IGNITE YOUR PASSION

178 FOREST AVE | OAK PARK, IL | 1PM TO 6PM
TICKETS: WWW.BIT.LY/BLACKGIRLPASSIONEVENT

PLEASE FOLLOW A GREAT WOMAN IN THE INDUSTRY SHE'S ON A MISSION TO PROVIDE GREAT SUPPORT FOR OTHERS IN THE INDUSTRY.

LETRISE CARTER IS A GREAT AUTHOR, MOTIVATOR, INSPIRATION AND SHE HAS PLATFORMS THAT WILL ASSIST YOU IN YOUR BUSINESS AS WELL.

FOLLOW HER ON FACEBOOK:

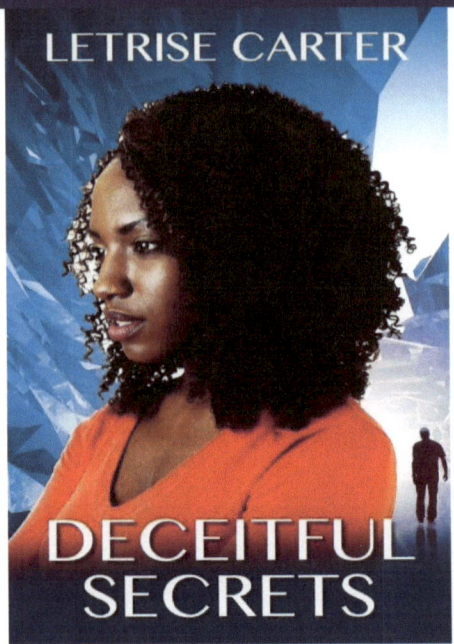

LETRISE CARTER

DECEITFUL SECRETS

THIS FAMILY IS ONE OF A KIND

"We don't give people any opportunity to find fault with how we serve, instead our lives demonstrate that we are God's servants. We have endured many things, suffering, distress, anxiety, beatings, imprisonments, riots, hard work, sleepless nights, and lack of food. People can see our purity, knowledge, patience, kindness, the Holy Spirit's presence in our lives, our sincere love, truthfulness, and the presence of God's power. We demonstrate that we are God's servants 2nd Corinthians 6:3-7"

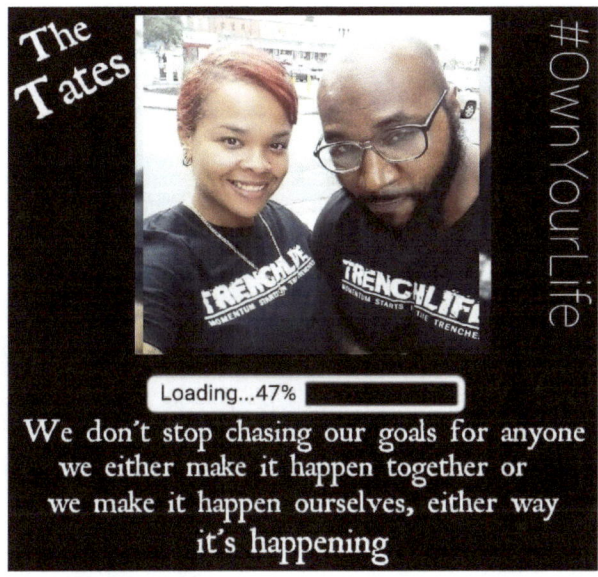

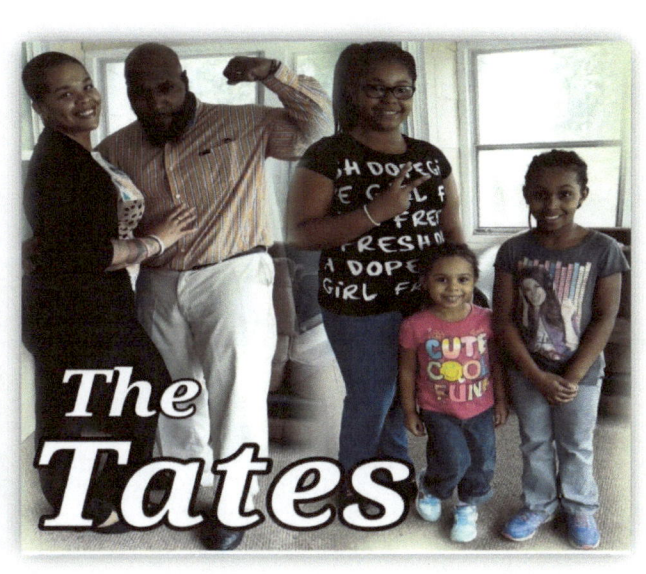

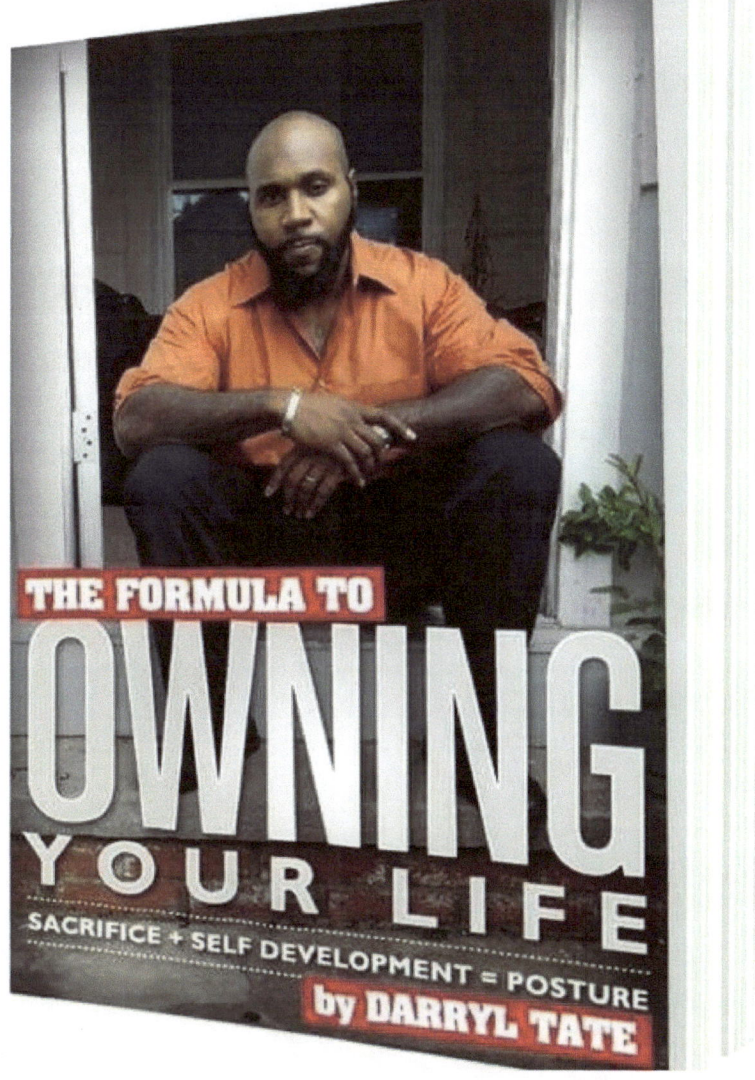

Follow: @1ofakindtate aka
#MrNoObjections #OwnYourLife

#TheTatesFromCleveland

AUTHORS ROCK!

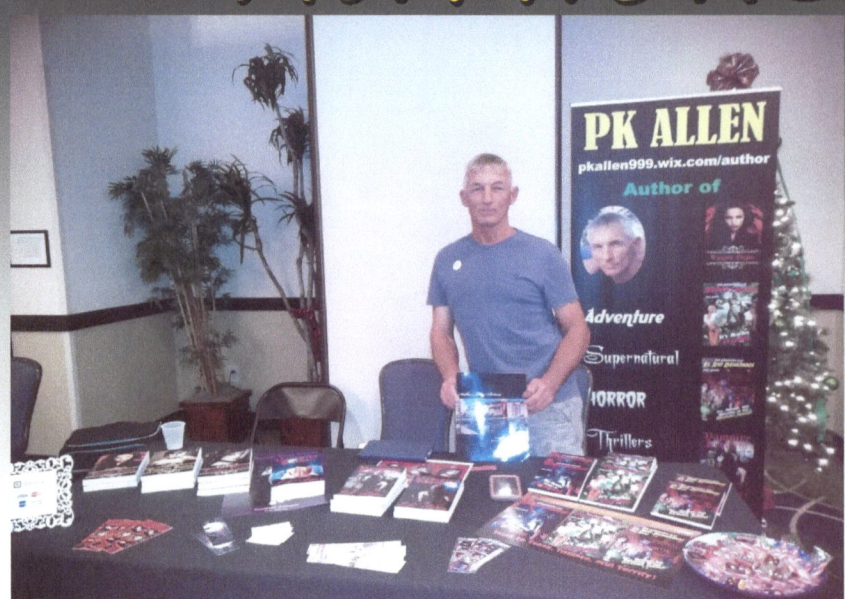

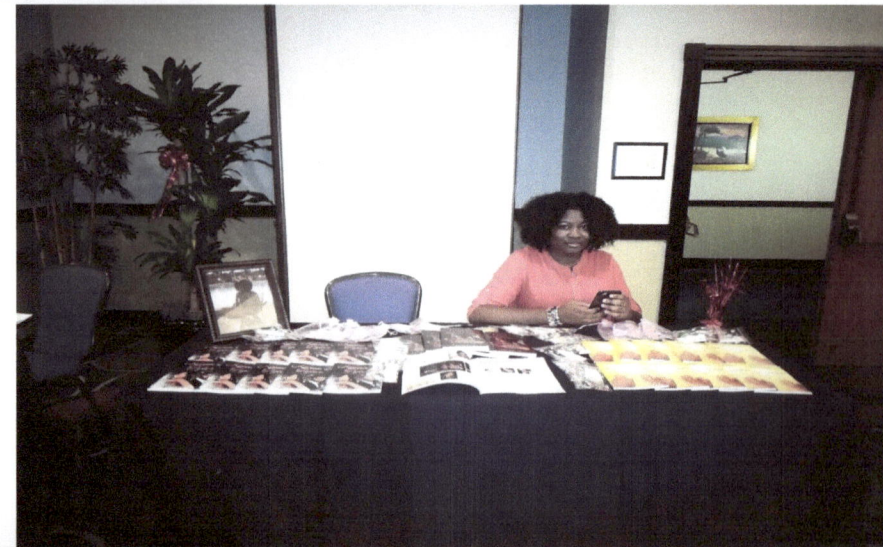

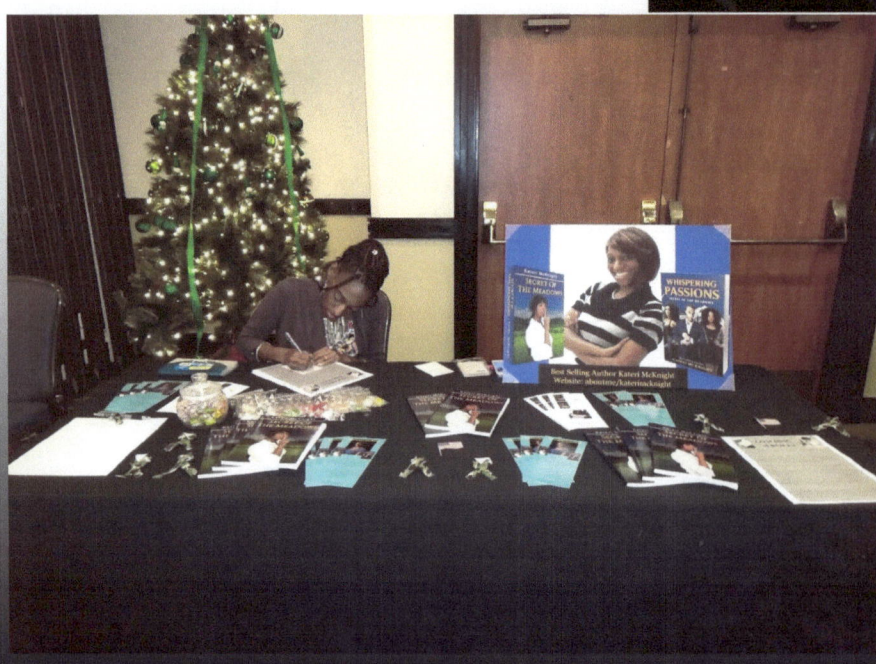

THe MiLK BaR
art bar

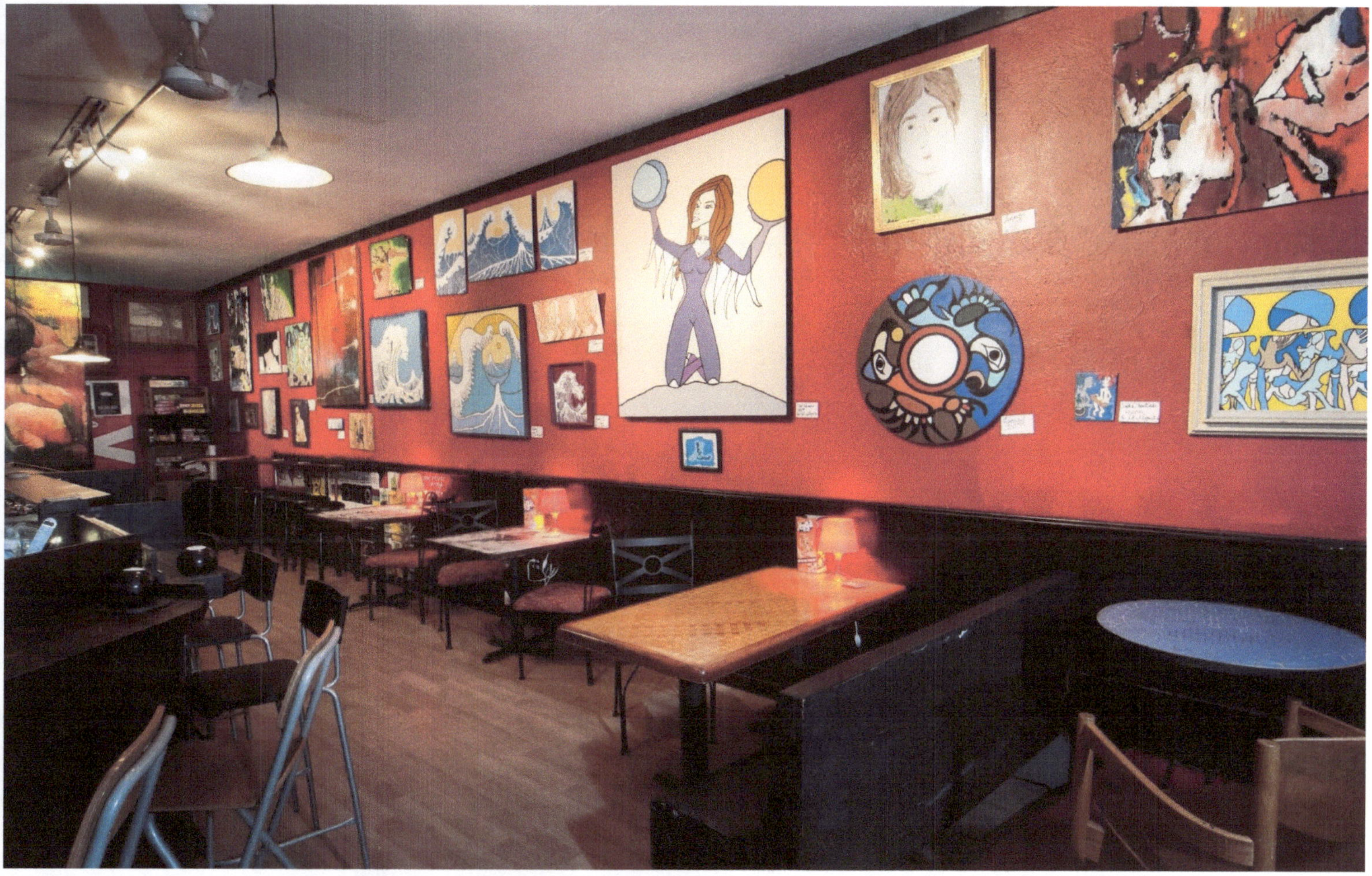

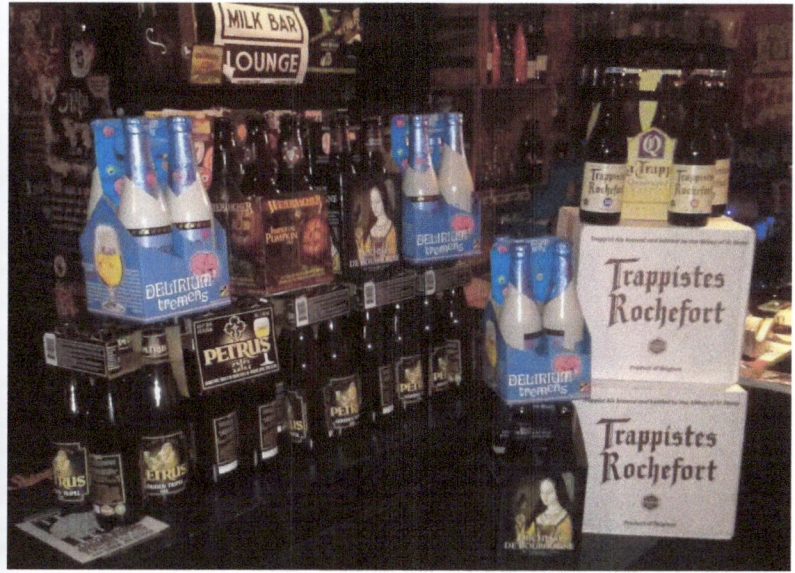

2424 E. Robinson St. Orlando, Florida 32803

(407) 440-8771

Hours: 6pm-1am

*ART *MUSIC *GREAT PERFORMANCES
*OPEN MIC

A GREAT SOCIAL SPOT THAT'S COZY &
LAID BACK

COME SEE FOR YOURSELF

PASTOR OF THE MONTH

Congratulations to Pastor Elder Fred Morris Jr. of First Trinity Free
Will Baptist Church located at 2141 Rock Quarry Rd. Raleigh, N.C. 27610

Pastor Morris was voted, August Pastor of the Month. Thank you The Light 103.9FM and Blue Cross & Blue Shield of NC

Accept Christ...It will lead you to anything you want.

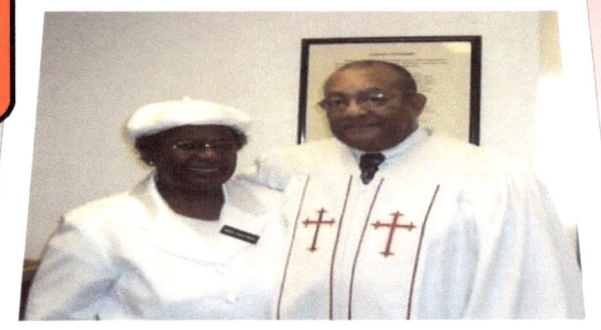

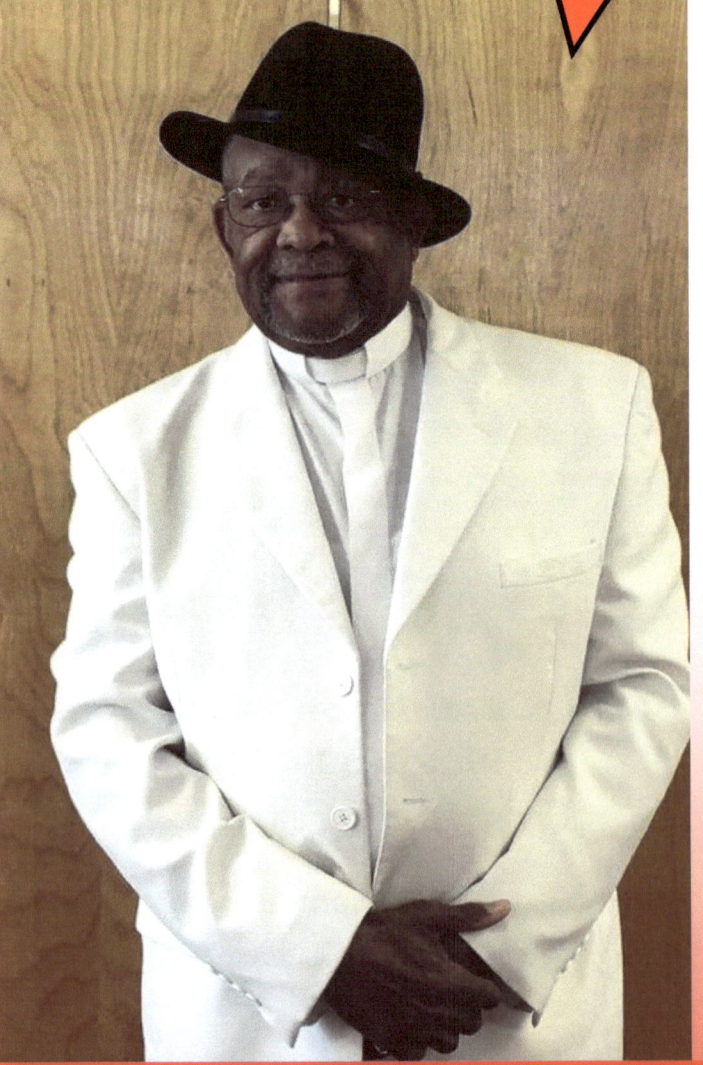

Elder Fred Morris is my dad, he has been the Pastor of First Trinity for 21 years. He just celebrated his Birthday and Pastoral anniversary in August. What a Blessed month he has had.

Elder Morris was the Deacon at Smith Temple Free Will Baptist Church prior to having his very own church. He has served as Assistant District Elder for Cape Fear Conference A in Erwin, N.C.

His congregation will tell you that he is a great leader, compassionate, and always takes extra time to visit nursing homes and hospitals with his wife.

He is also know for taking extra time out to minister to the homeless and those that are less fortunate.

That's my daddy, my Role Model, my Mentor.

By Loretta Morris-White

Elder Morris is the husband of Lenora P. Morris for 56 years. They are the parents of 4 daughters and 1 son, 12 grandchildren, 6 great grandchildren and 2 great great grands.

#WERAP4VETS

Veterans should be recognized everyday not just once a year. As a Veteran, Loretta has experienced so many obstacles along with many other Veterans. While living in a Homeless transitional housing program with Veterans; she was one woman among 70 + men who have served this country and ended up HOMELESS. Loretta had become a voice for the Veterans but now realizes that it will take more than one voice to be heard. "We are seeking Performers that would like to assist us on our mission to be a voice for the Veterans by utilizing their voices to produce great, positive and inspirational music."

Please contact us at: jazzyartzmagazine1@gmail.com if you would like to Sponsor, Donate or Participate.

REMEMBER: WE ARE FREE BECAUSE OF THE BRAVE!

ADVOCATING FOR OUR VETERANS

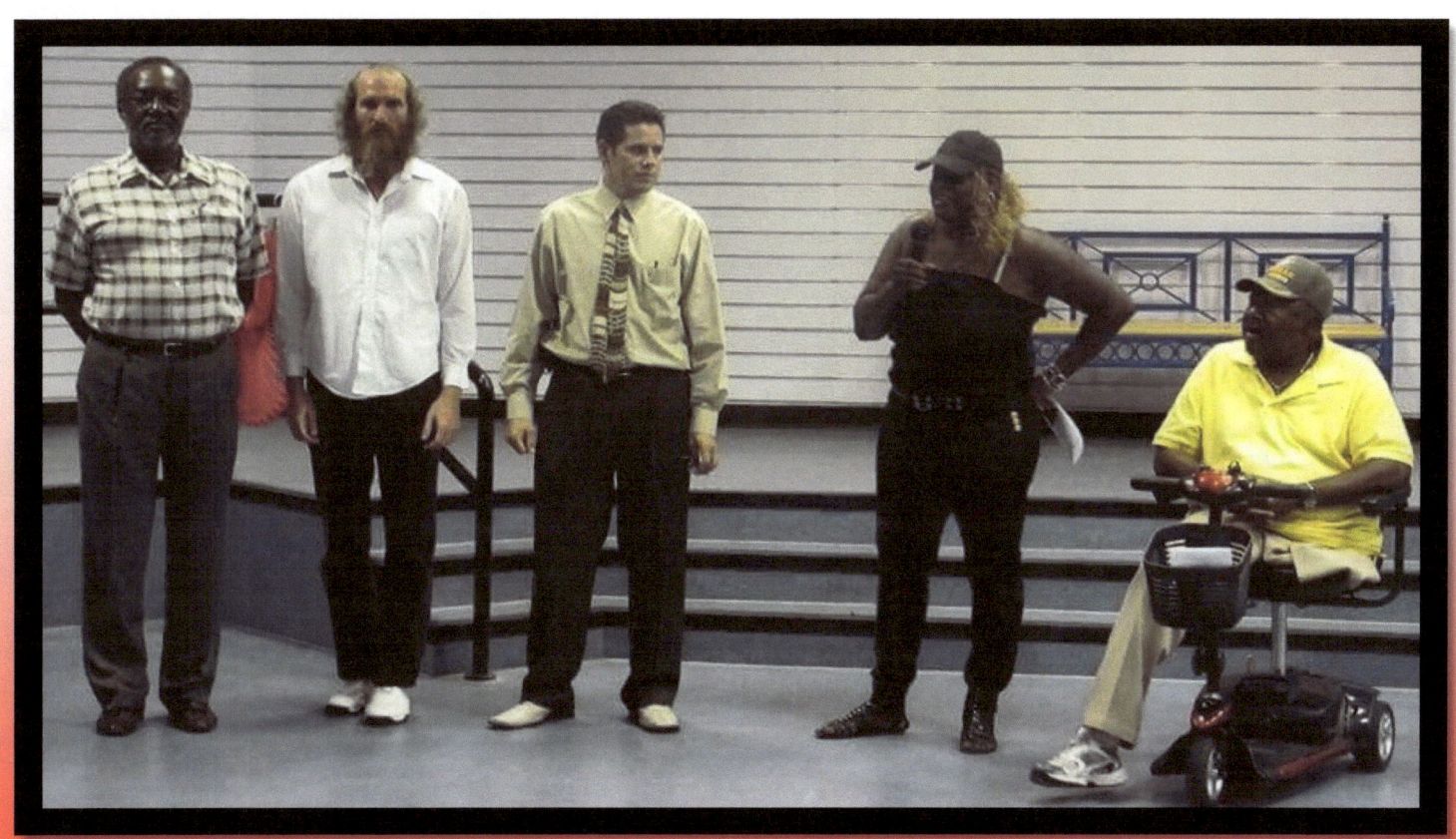

COMMUNITY HEROES

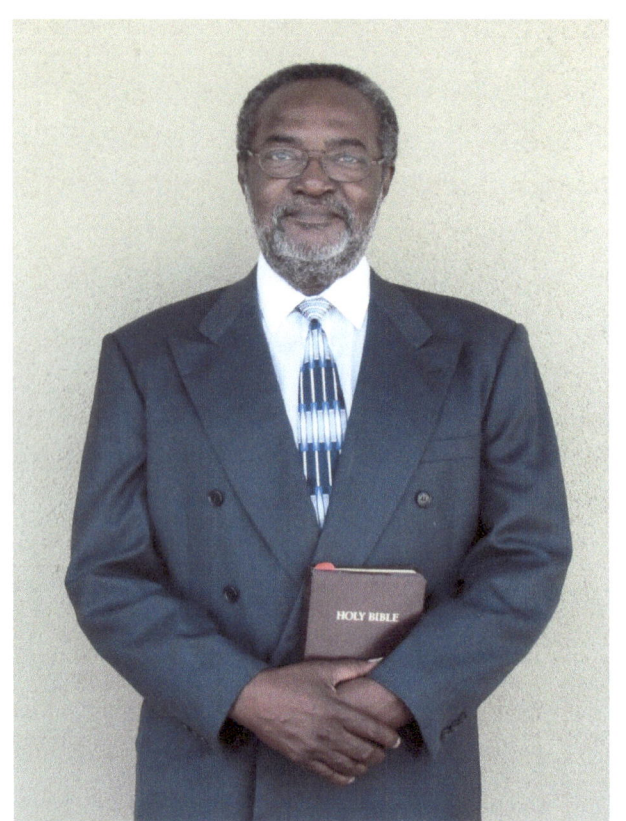

Clyde Baker, a U.S. Army Veteran, continues to serve the communities.

HE HAS A SAYING AND A VERSE THAT HE LIVES BY...

"BE STILL AND KNOW THAT I AM GOD!"

Mr. Clyde Baker is a Mentor, great Role Model and a brother to many young men.

Mr. Baker has assisted in the community with providing the Performing Arts. He has played main characters in a couple of Stage Play productions. He has been a great Mentor for a group of children and their school that is located in Kenya, Africa.

Mr. Clyde Baker is also a Retiree of the Kennedy Space Center in Florida.

VETERANS

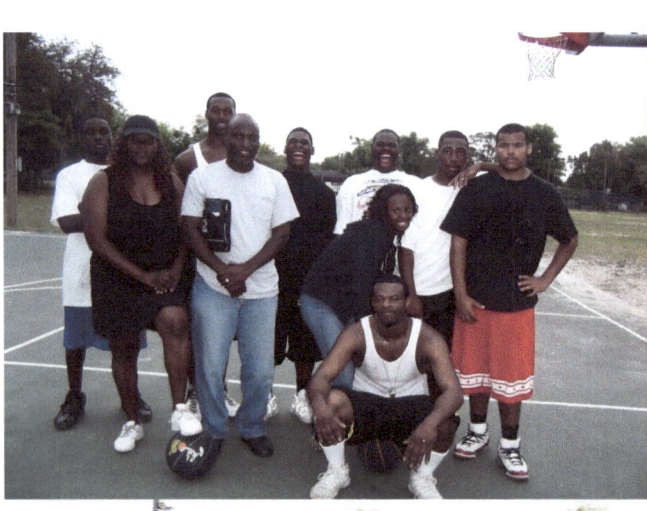

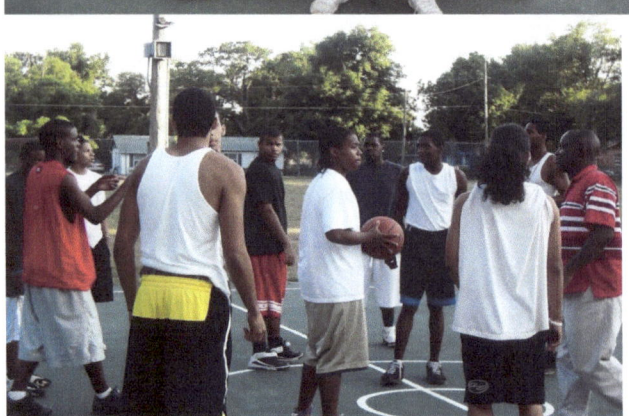

Paul Francis has done it all. He is a U.S. Navy Veteran. He continues to serve the community in whatever aspect he is called to do. He has worked with all ages, races and religions. No matter what is needed of him, he believes that God will absolutely give him the time and energy to do it.

He has a saying that he will leave everywhere that he goes...

BLESS YO HEART!

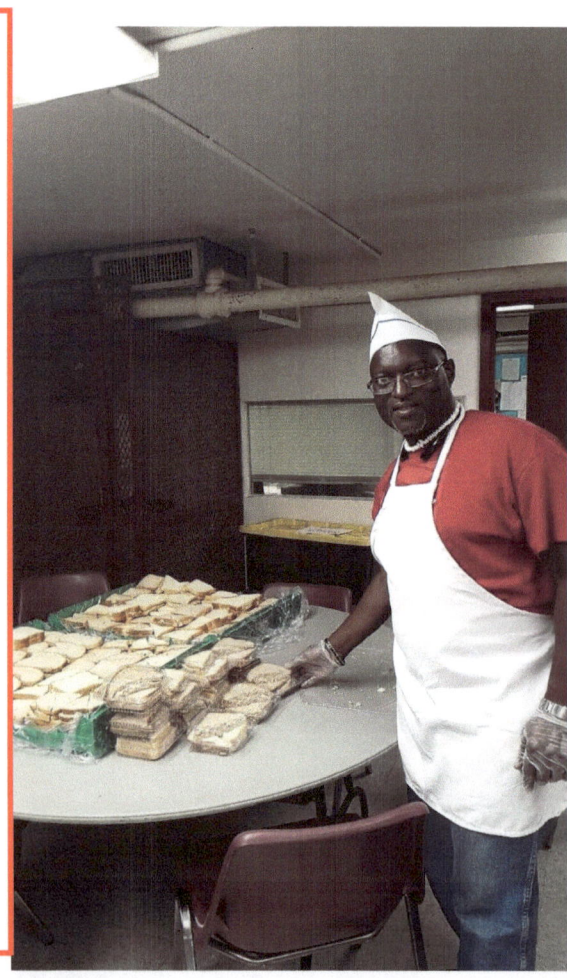

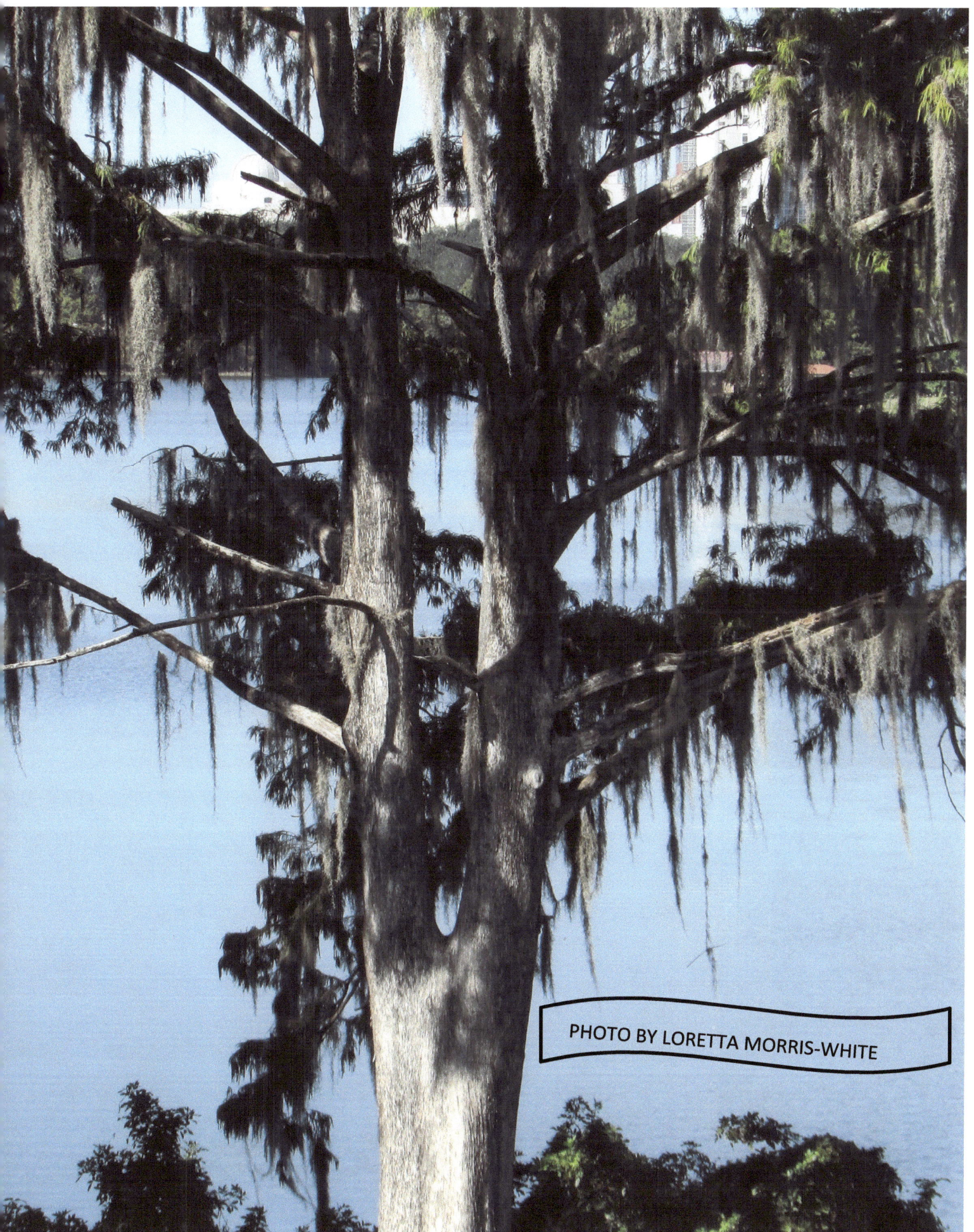

PHOTO BY LORETTA MORRIS-WHITE

GRAFFITI JUNKTION

American Burger Bar

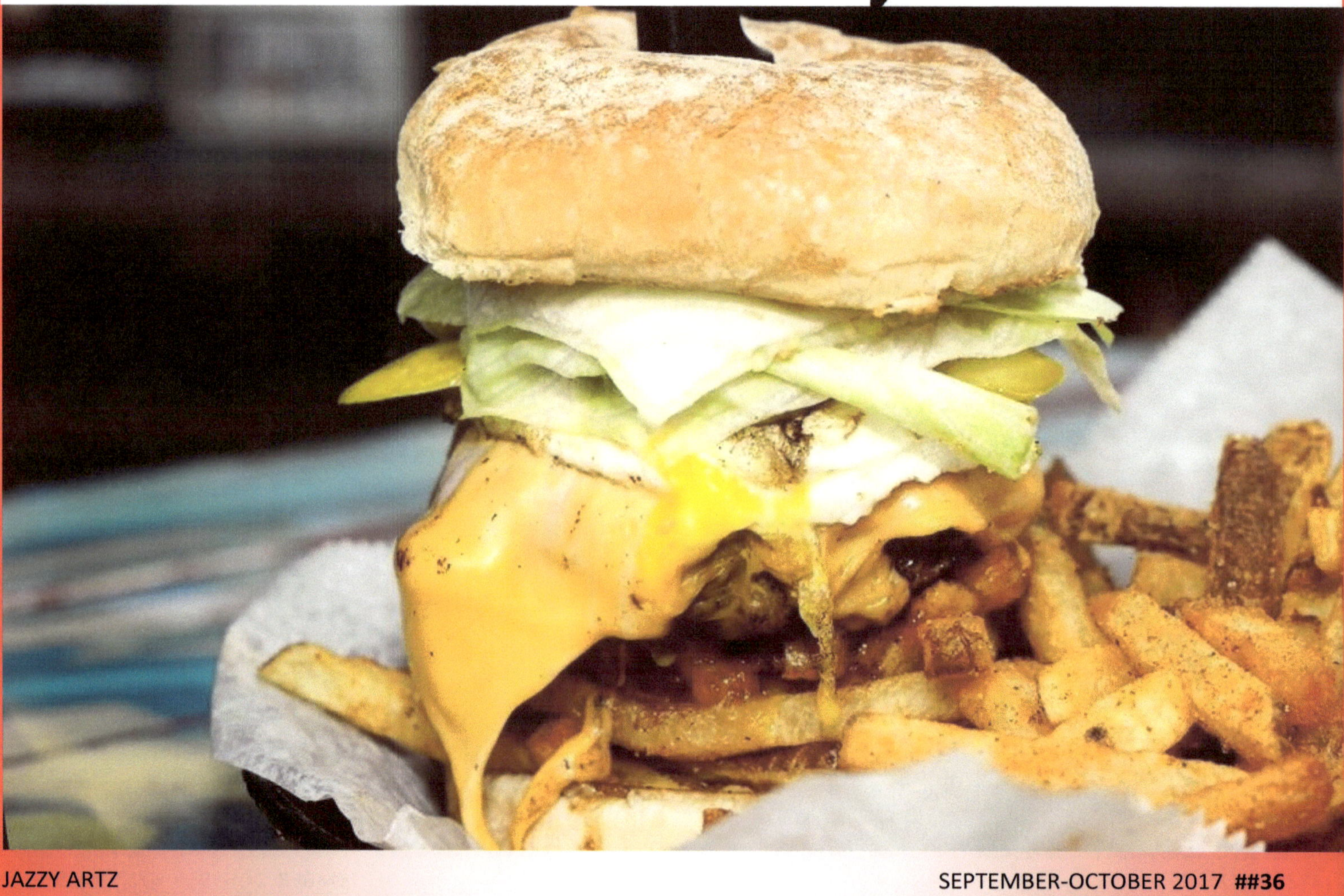

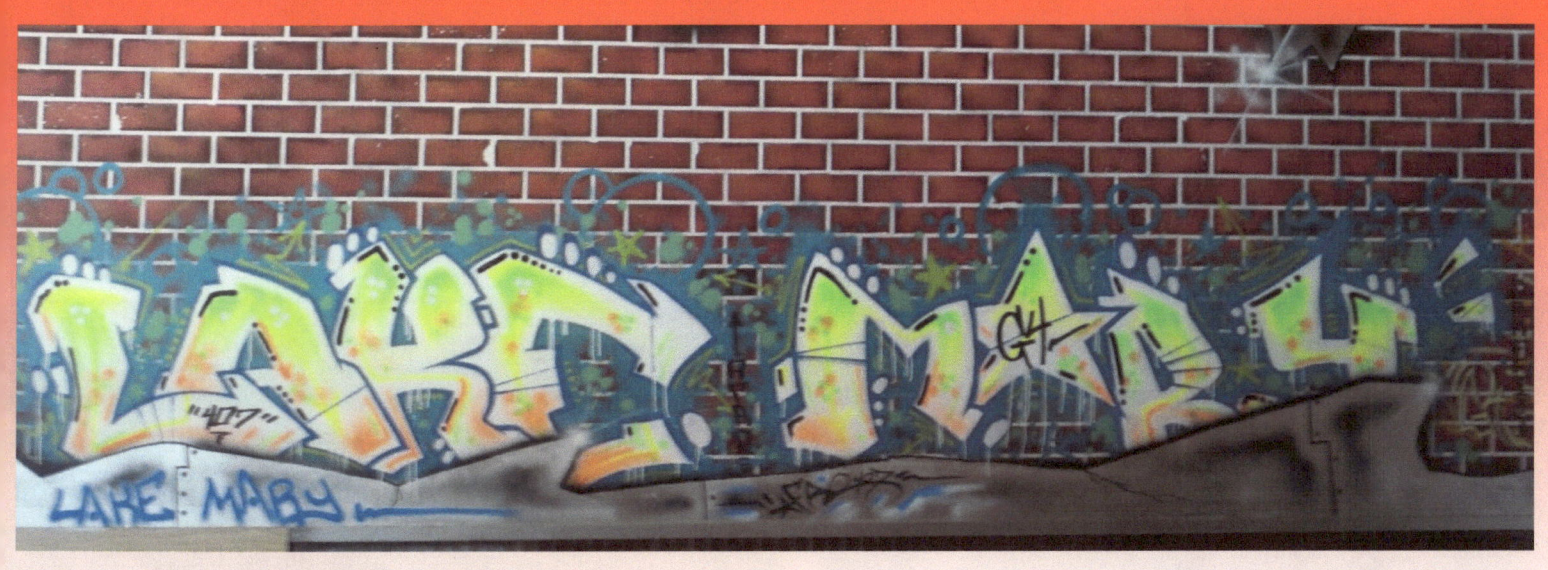

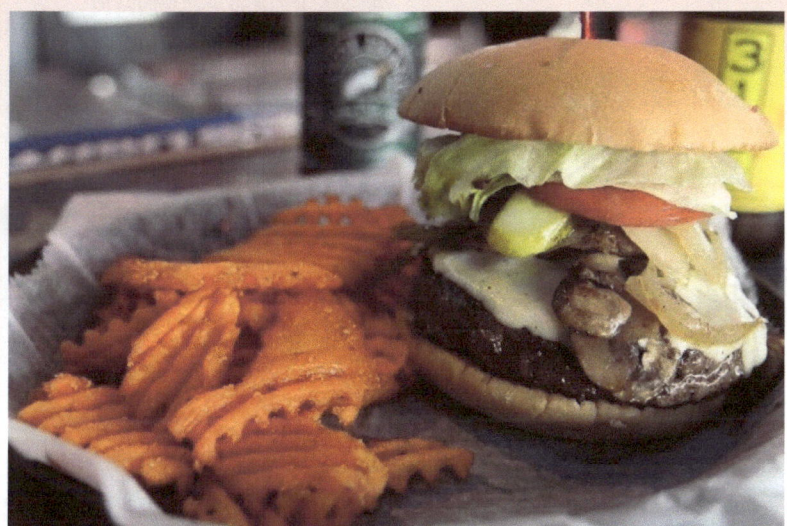

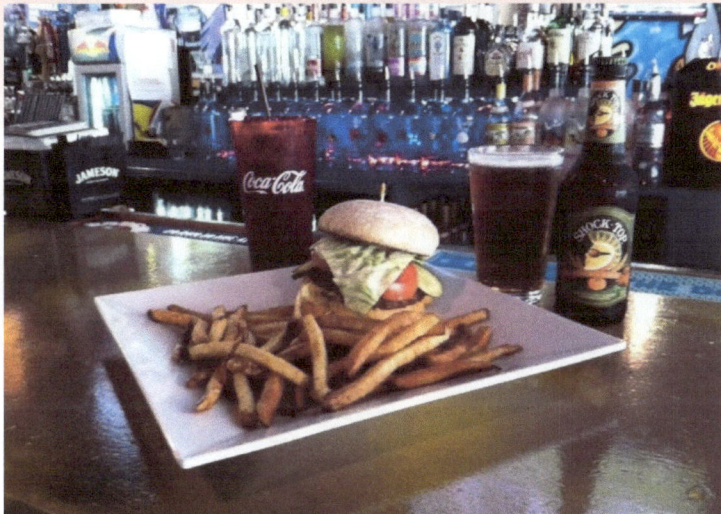

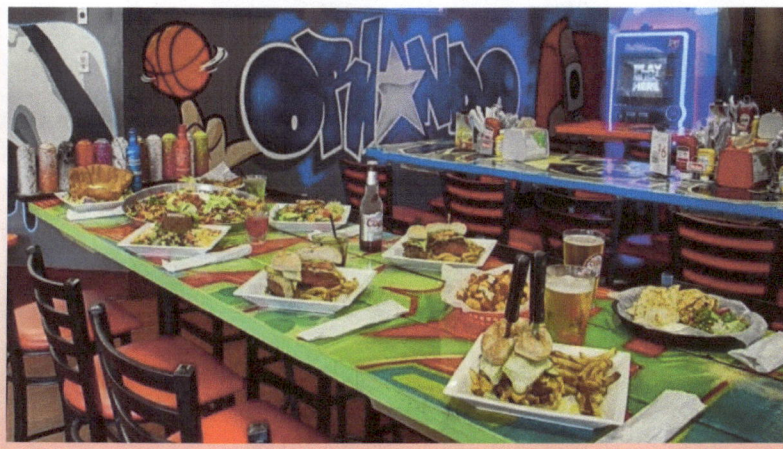

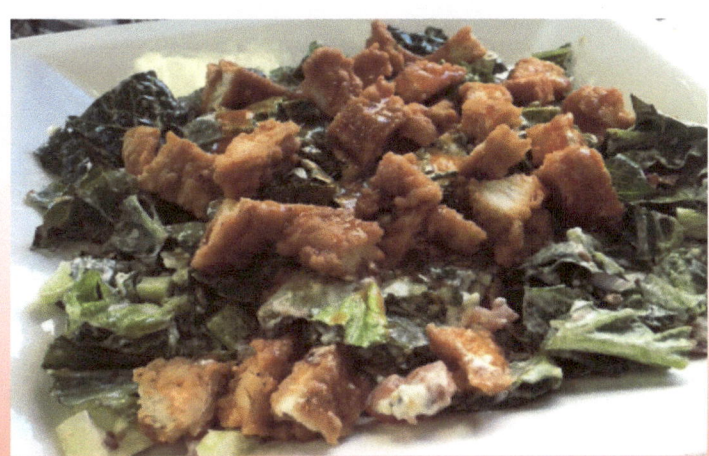

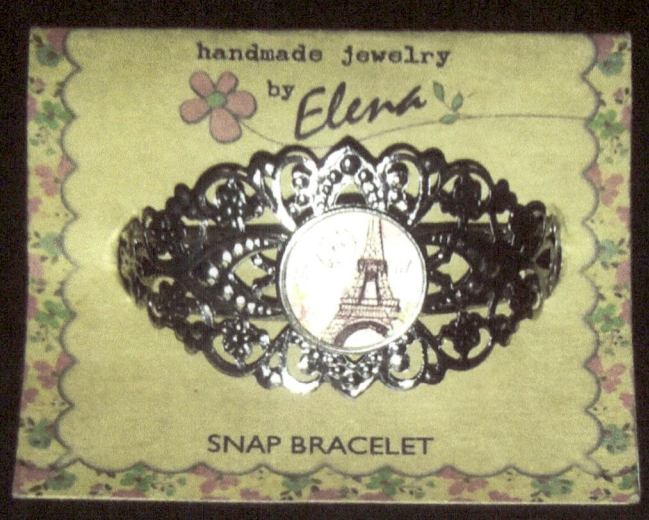

SNAP BRACELET

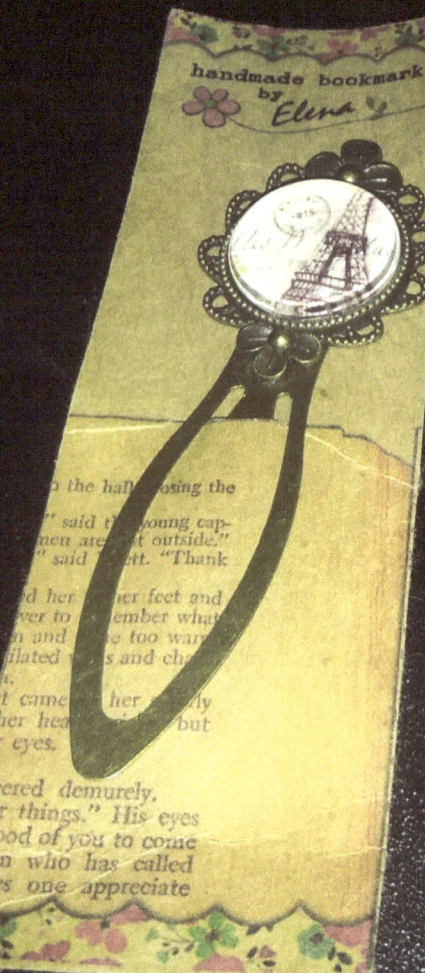

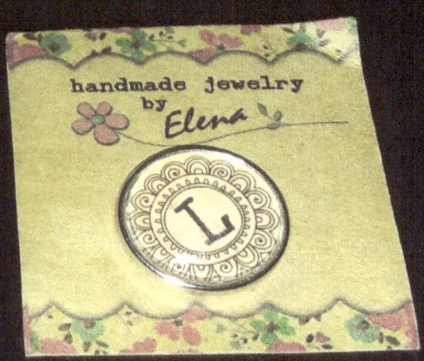

HANDCRAFTED JEWELRY

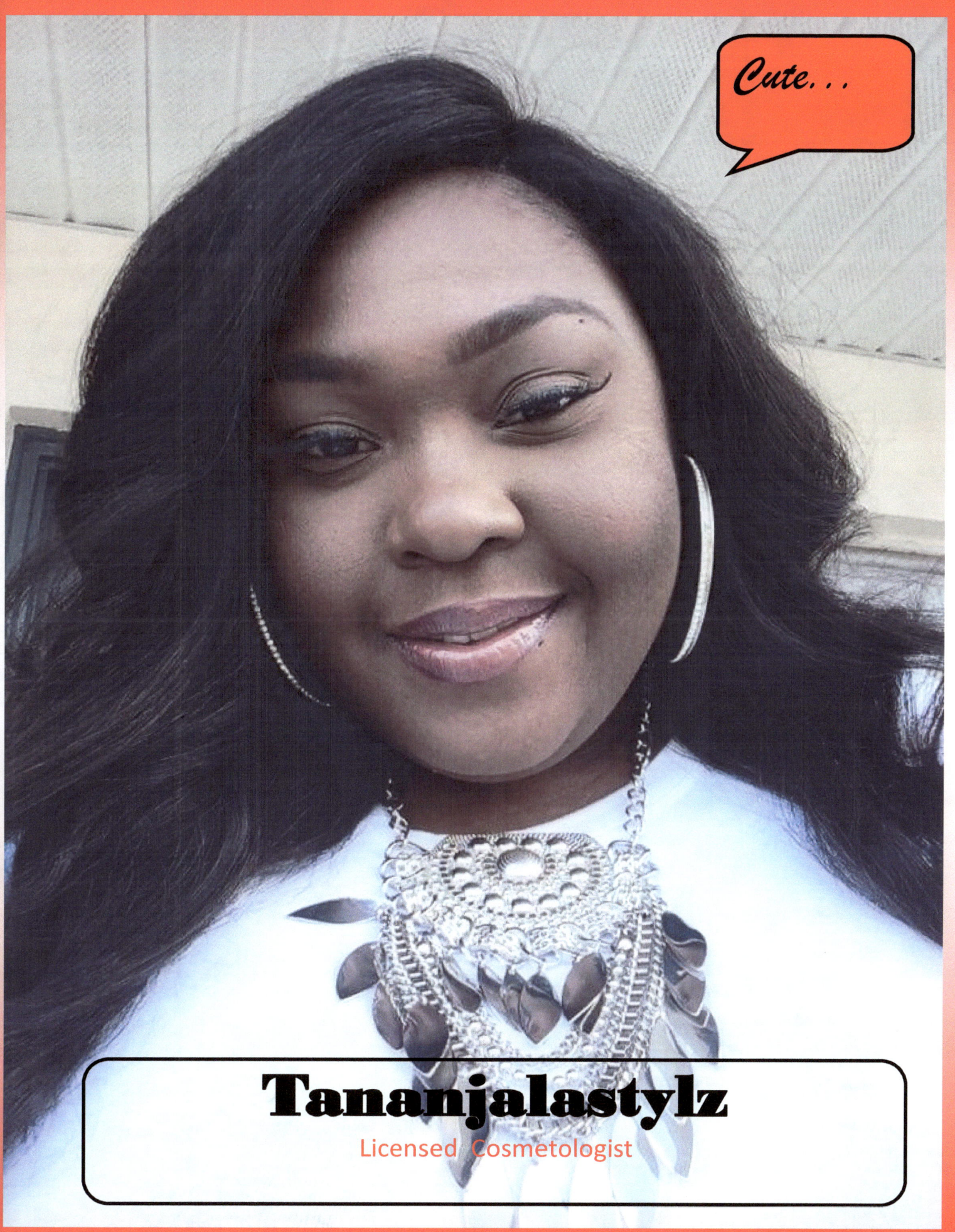

Cute...

Tananjalastylz
Licensed Cosmetologist

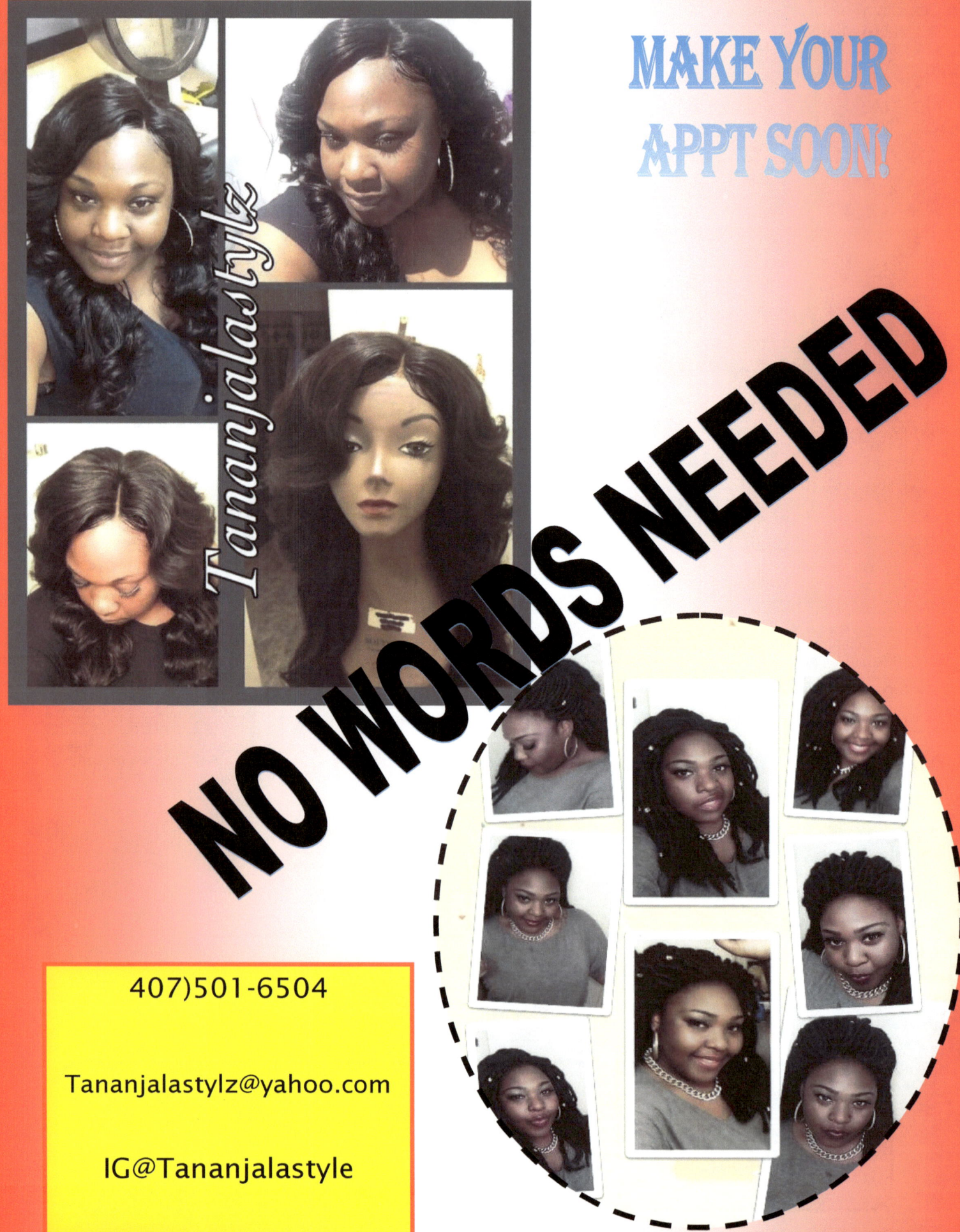

MAKE YOUR APPT SOON!

NO WORDS NEEDED

Tananjalastylz

407)501-6504

Tananjalastylz@yahoo.com

IG@Tananjalastyle

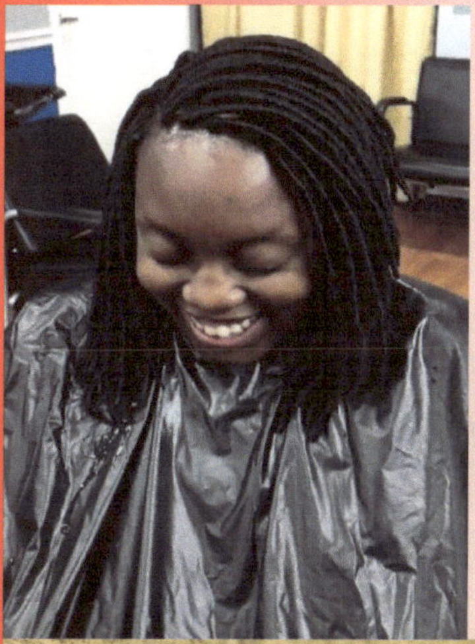

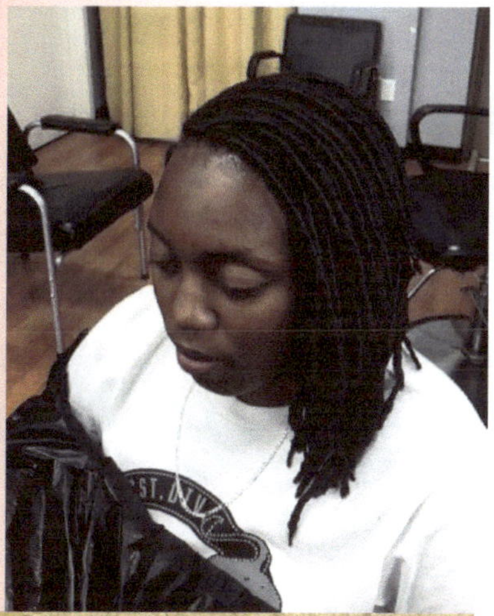

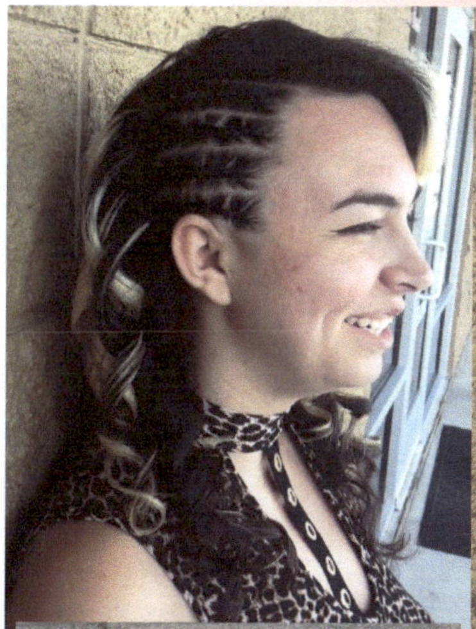

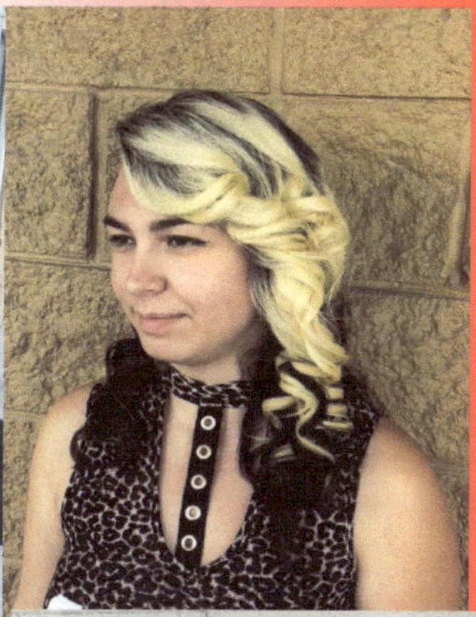

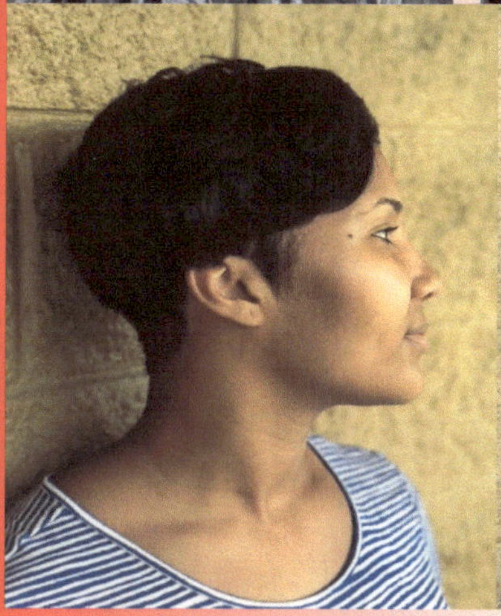

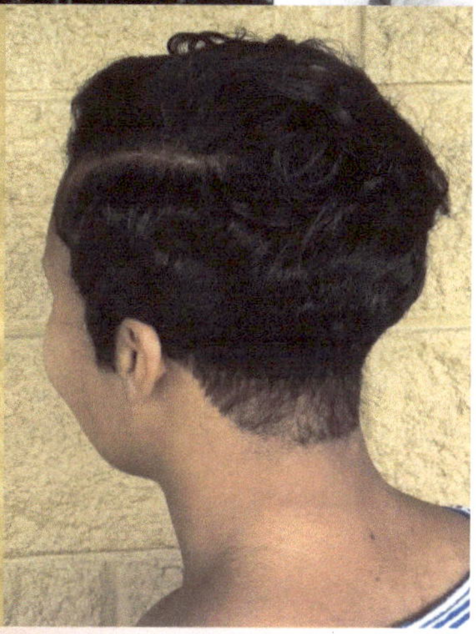

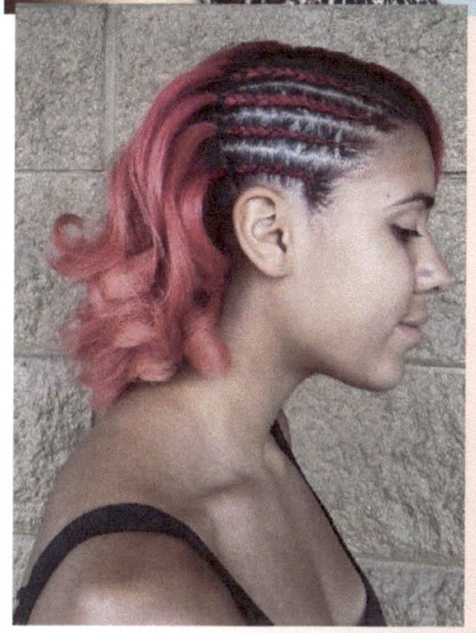

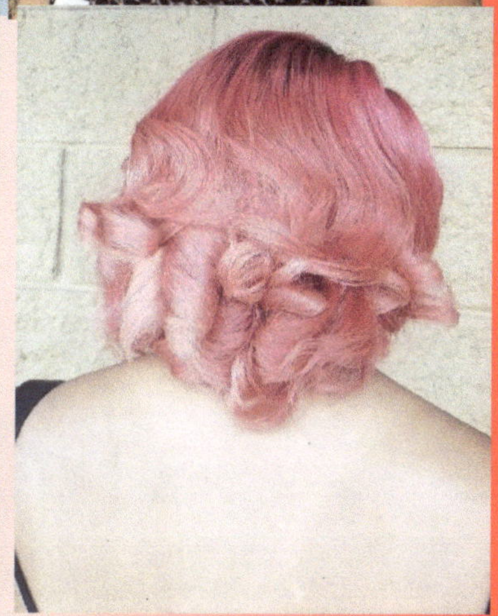

SERVING CENTRAL FLORIDA

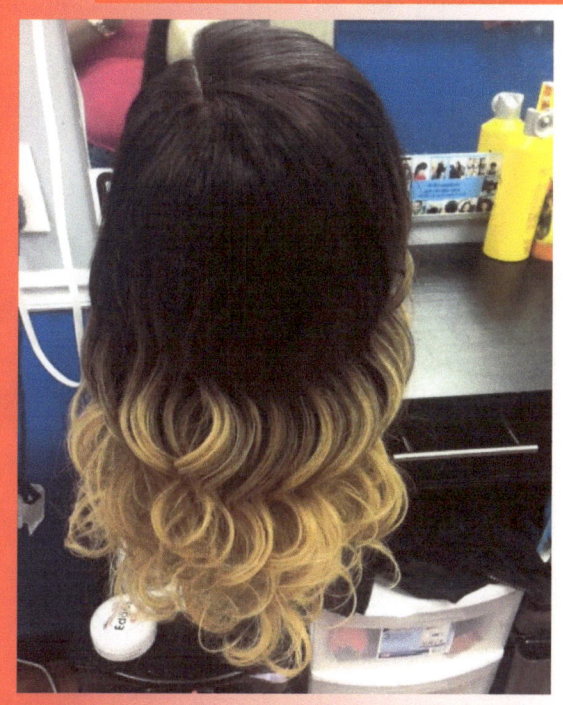

WIGS
COLORS
CUTS
WEAVES
&
MORE

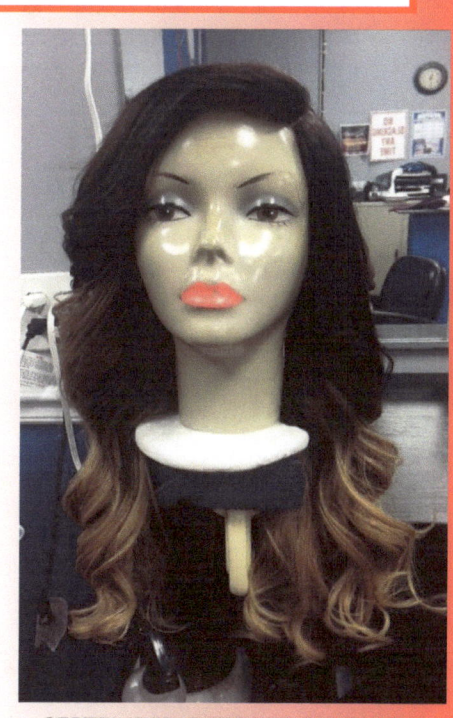

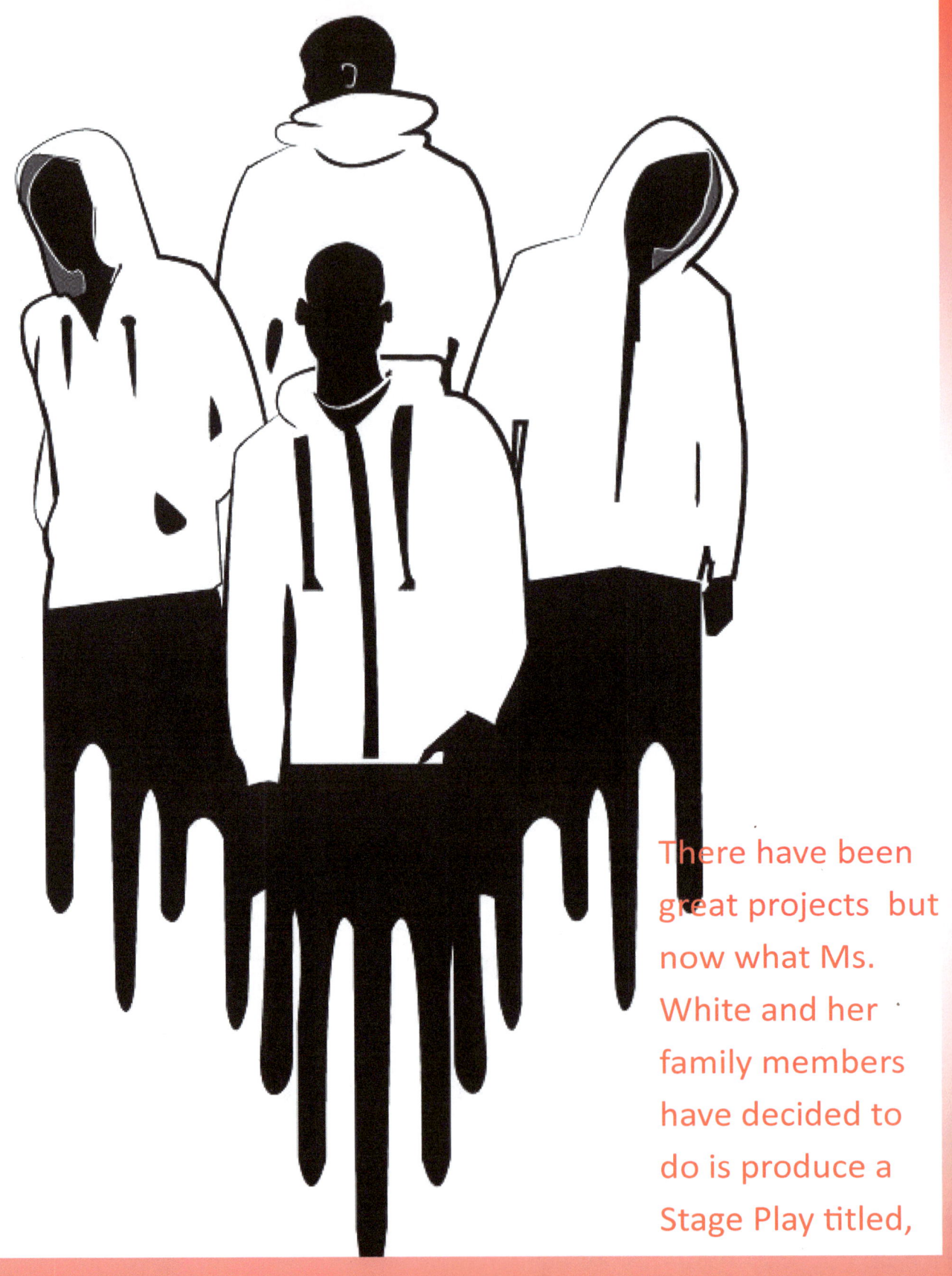

There have been great projects but now what Ms. White and her family members have decided to do is produce a Stage Play titled,

Why Did I Have to Die?

Why Did I Have to Die?

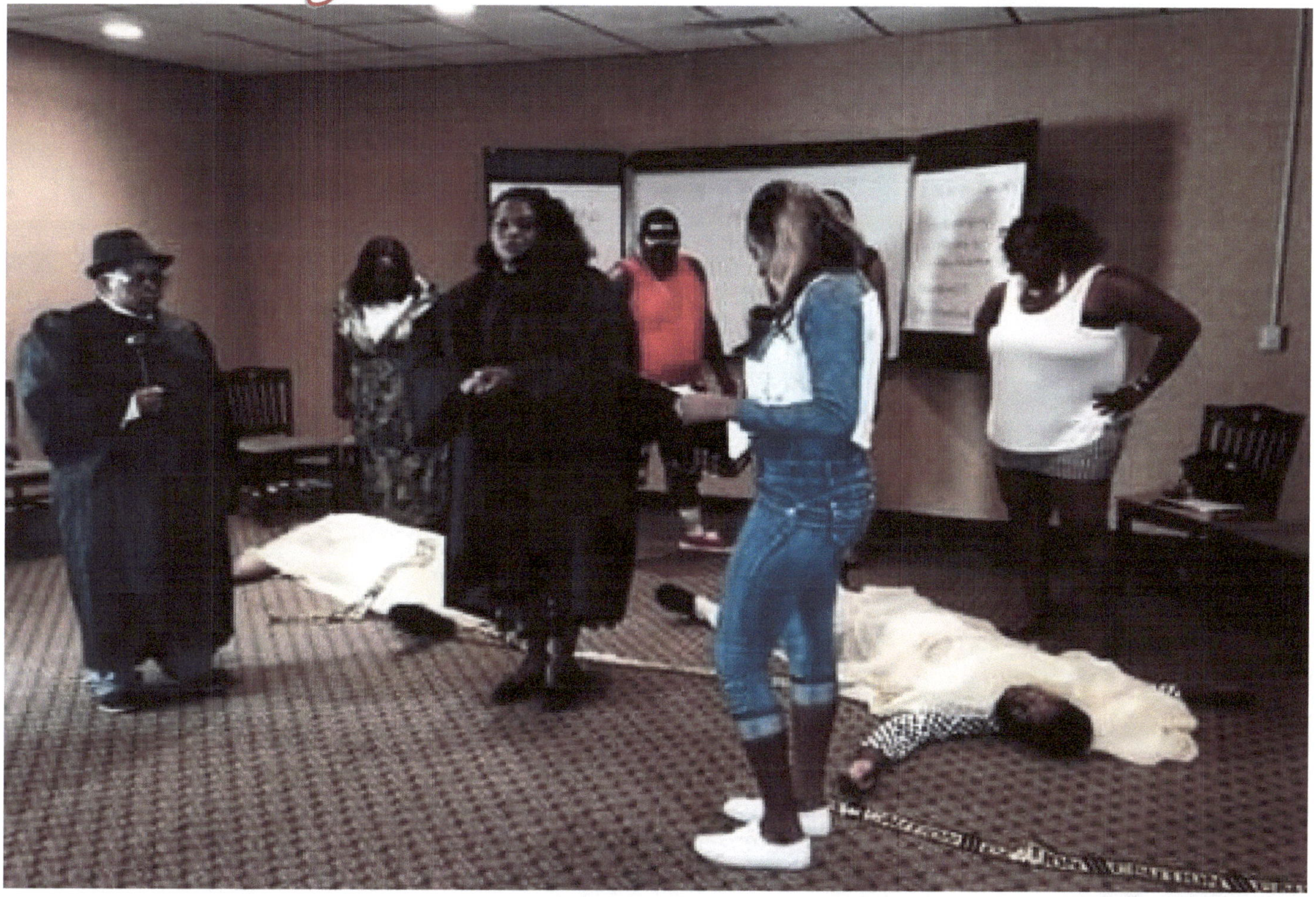

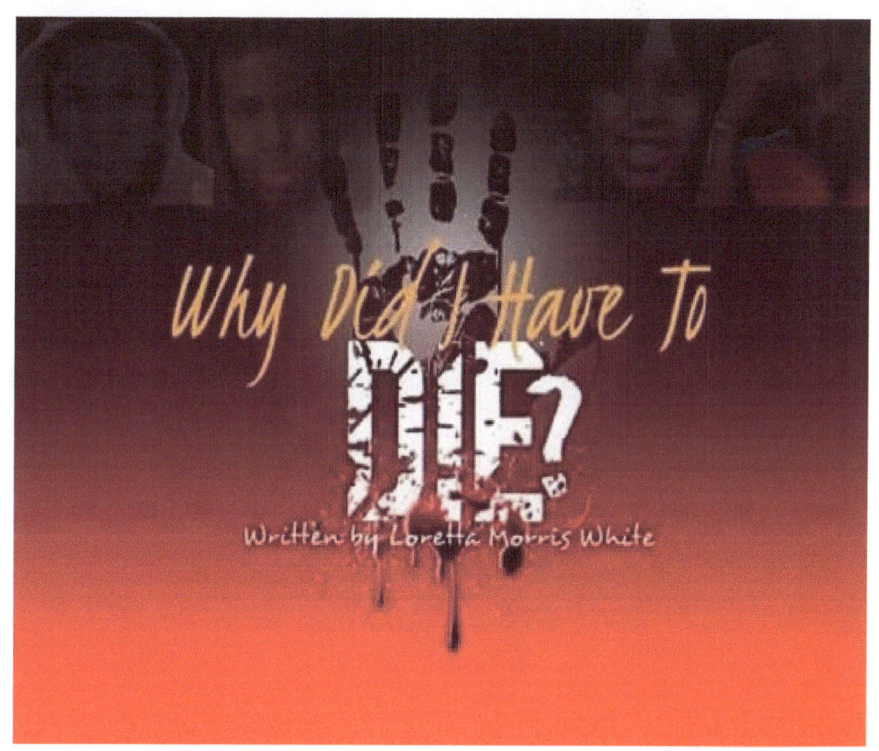

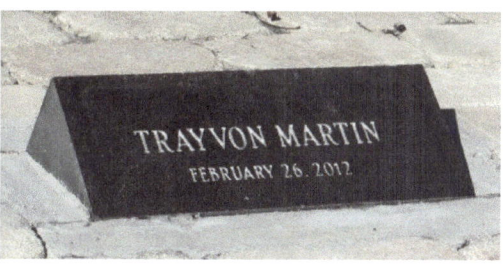

In 2012 a major tragedy struck that touched the entire U.S. It was the murder of a teenager. Now mind you, this was not the first teen that had been murdered before but there was something different about this case. Now at the time, I was living in Sanford, Florida across from the Courthouse that the trial was held. I had to relive this event practically everyday. I had to do something. So I decided to write a Stage play, in order for people to see this hurt and pain live.-Loretta Morris White

We really want to know why? Every day we are loosing a child. Is this natural? Now a days, the parents are outliving their children. What is that saying? Why? Why are our children dying?

We have got to Save Our Sons

There are so many organizations starting programs and people from around the world are trying to come up with solutions. But guess what? The killings are not stopping! What is the reason for this change in our society?

S.O.S.

Family

School

Church

Community

Friends

We need to see how this crime is changing our world.

- Why is there youth on youth crime?

- There is not just certain communities, or certain races or religions. There are killings everywhere.

- Why is there so much hate among our youth?

    - There are more bullying here with everyone.

We have got to stop talking!

...And starting doing.

kat korner

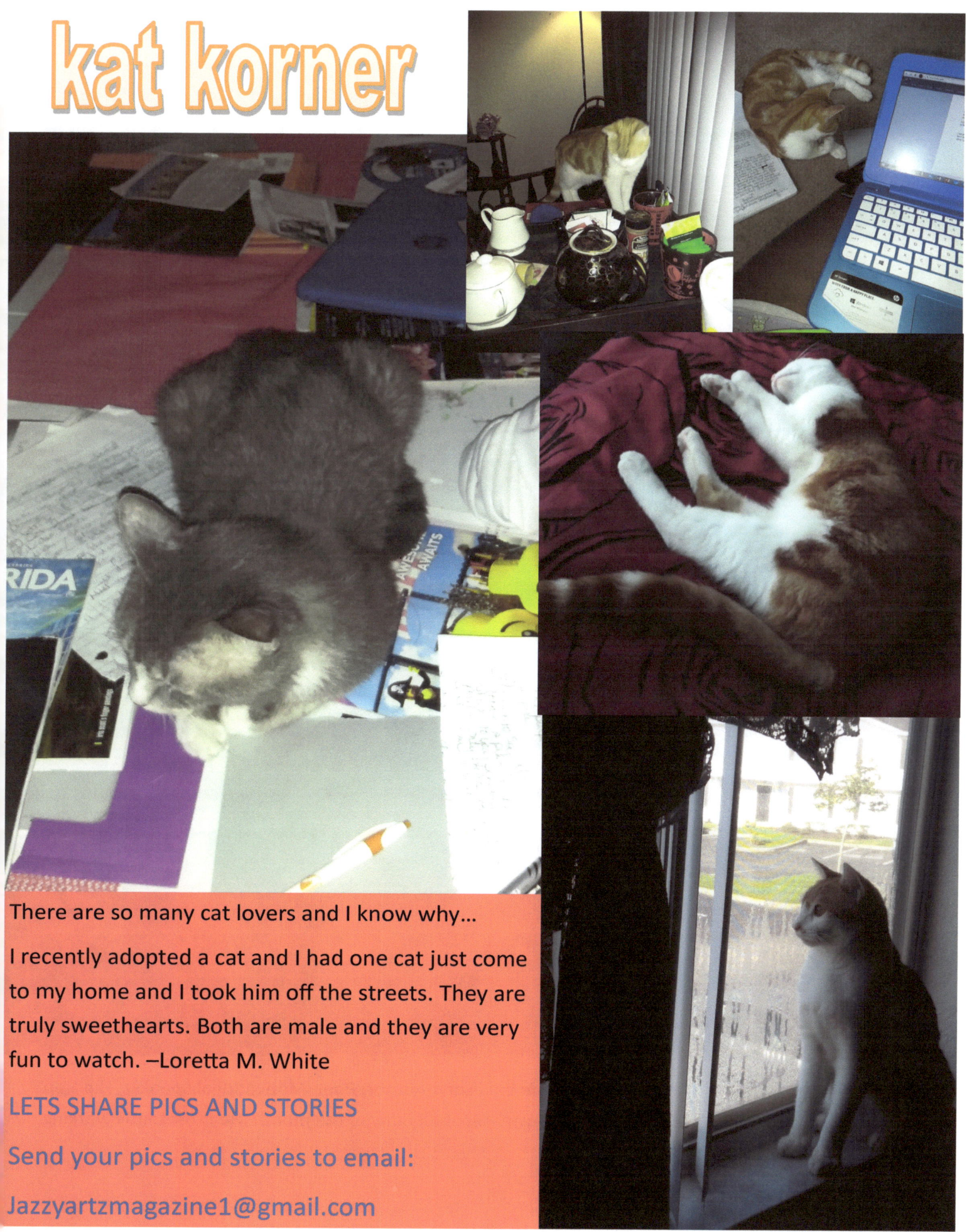

There are so many cat lovers and I know why...

I recently adopted a cat and I had one cat just come to my home and I took him off the streets. They are truly sweethearts. Both are male and they are very fun to watch. —Loretta M. White

LETS SHARE PICS AND STORIES

Send your pics and stories to email:

Jazzyartzmagazine1@gmail.com

A CLASS ACT!

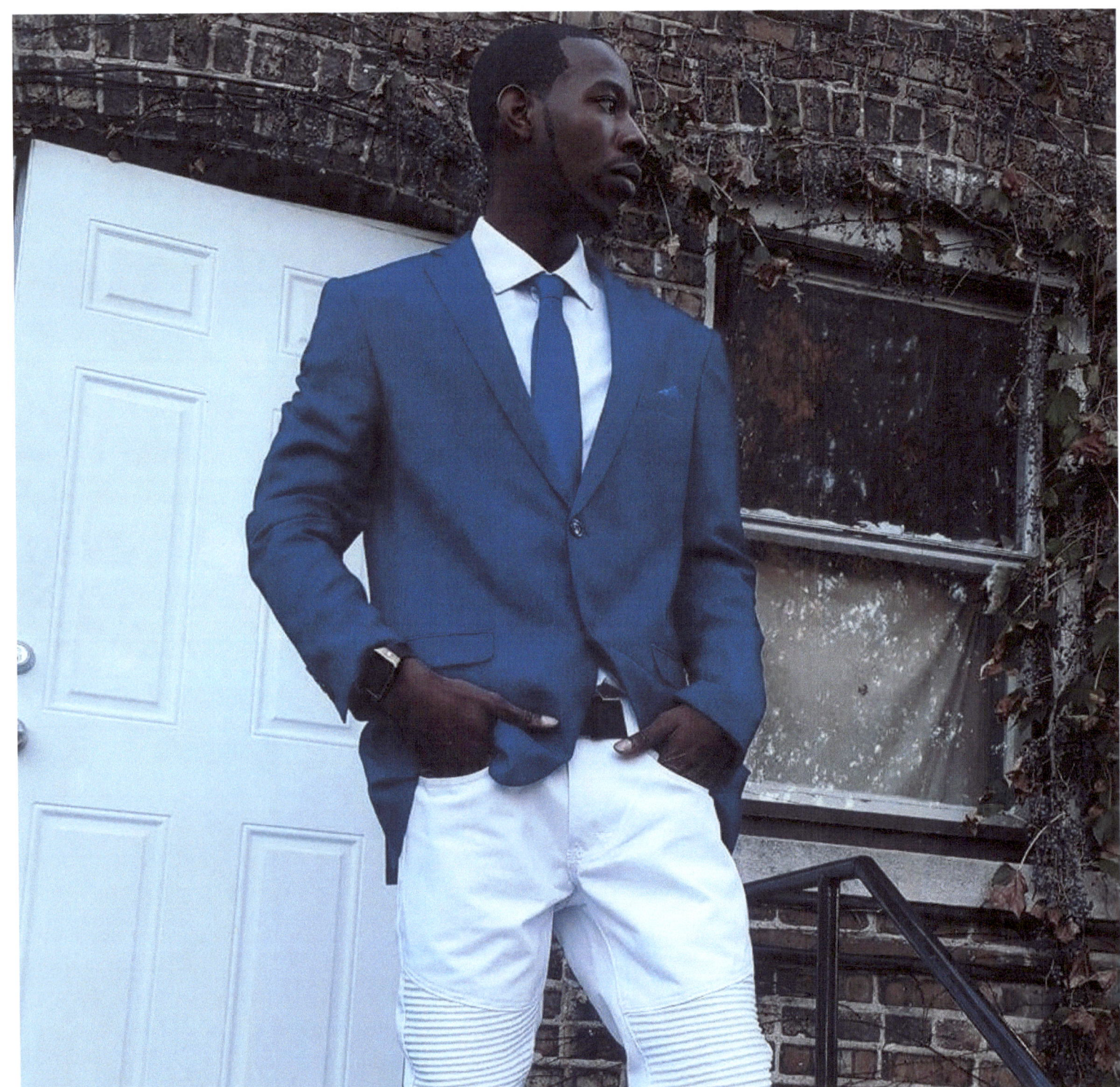

Mr. Markell Kells Thompson is an awesome Published Author, Poet, Motivational Speaker, Hip Hop Artist and Host of his very own Open Mic set every second Friday of the month. He is presently working on his second book and CD.

You can follow him on Facebook, and Instagram @kellstheartist

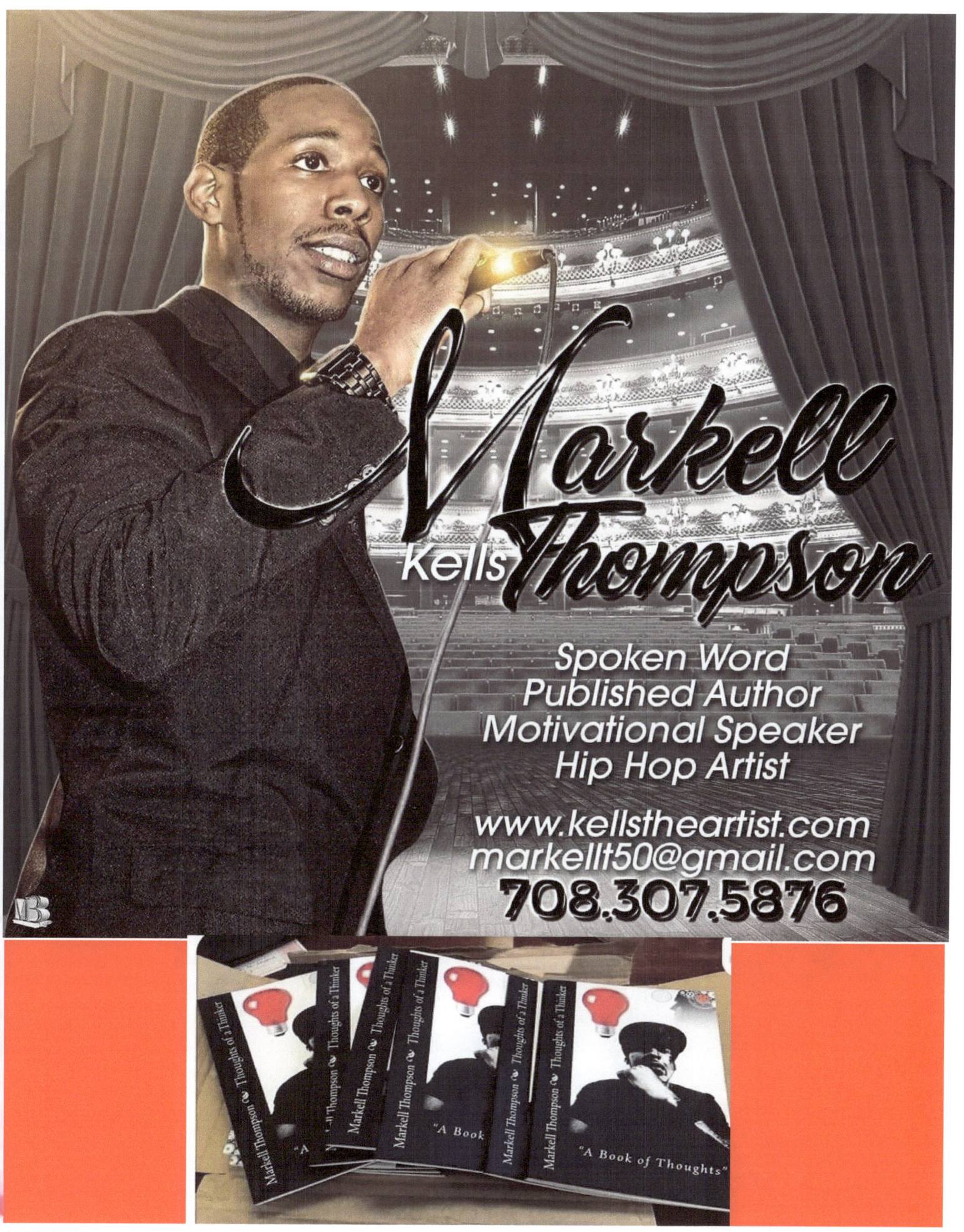

Markell
Kells Thompson

Spoken Word
Published Author
Motivational Speaker
Hip Hop Artist

www.kellstheartist.com
markellt50@gmail.com
708.307.5876

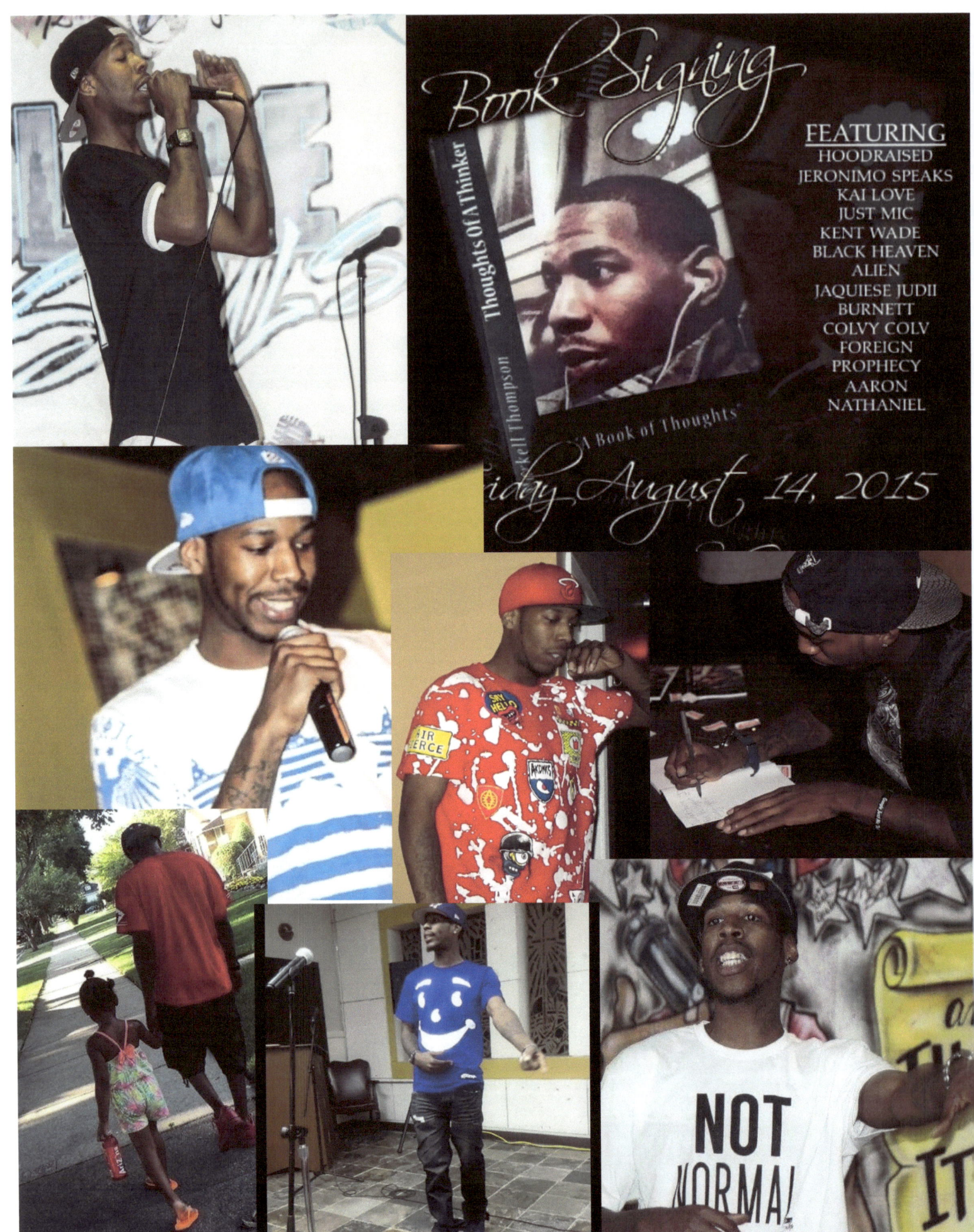

Book Signing

FEATURING
HOODRAISED
JERONIMO SPEAKS
KAI LOVE
JUST MIC
KENT WADE
BLACK HEAVEN
ALIEN
JAQUIESE JUDII
BURNETT
COLVY COLV
FOREIGN
PROPHECY
AARON
NATHANIEL

Thoughts Of A Thinker

"A Book of Thoughts"

Friday August 14, 2015

the beauty of it all

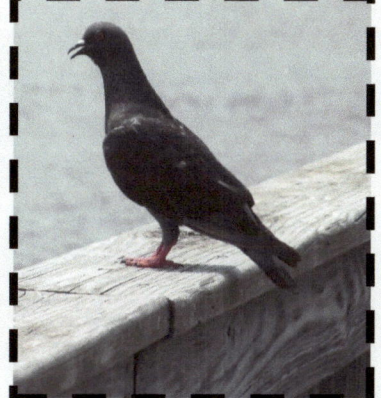
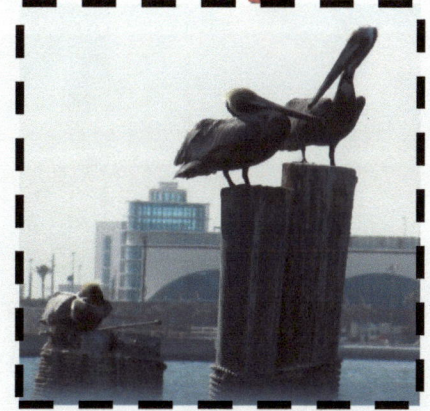
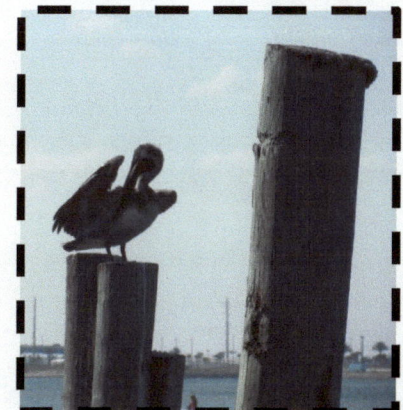

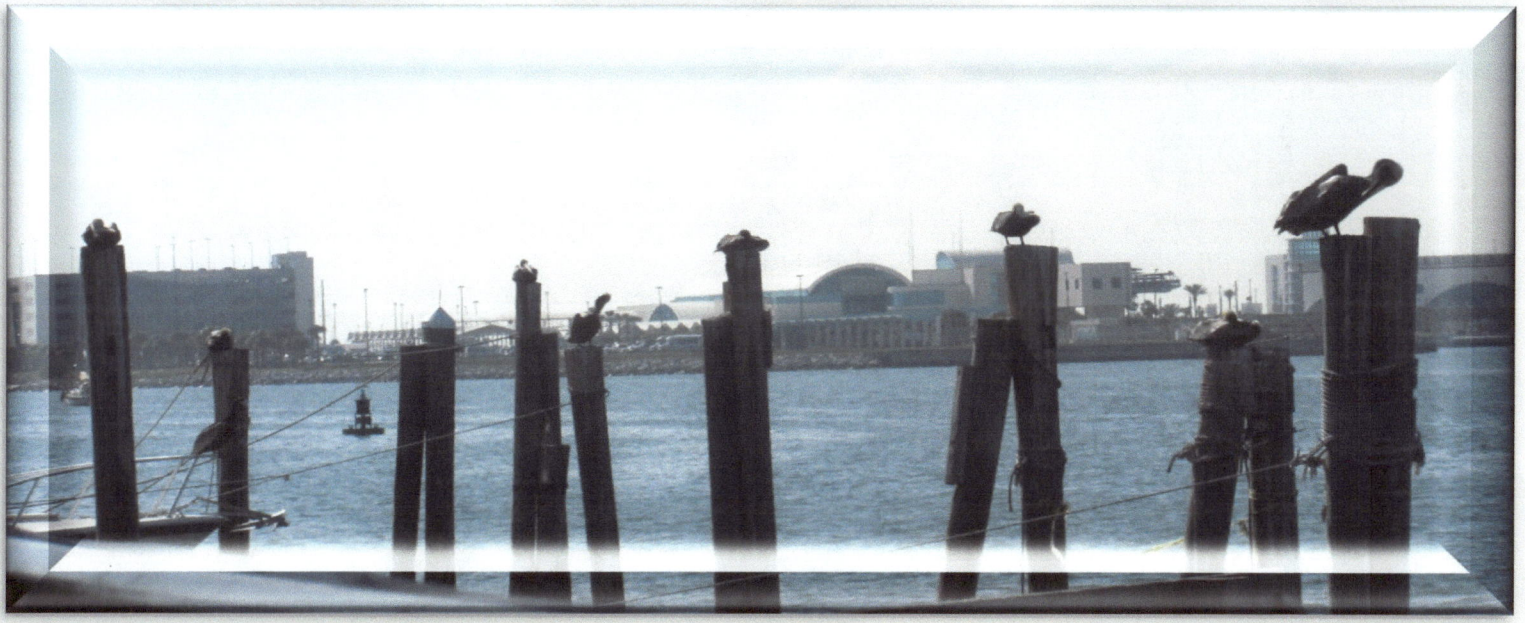

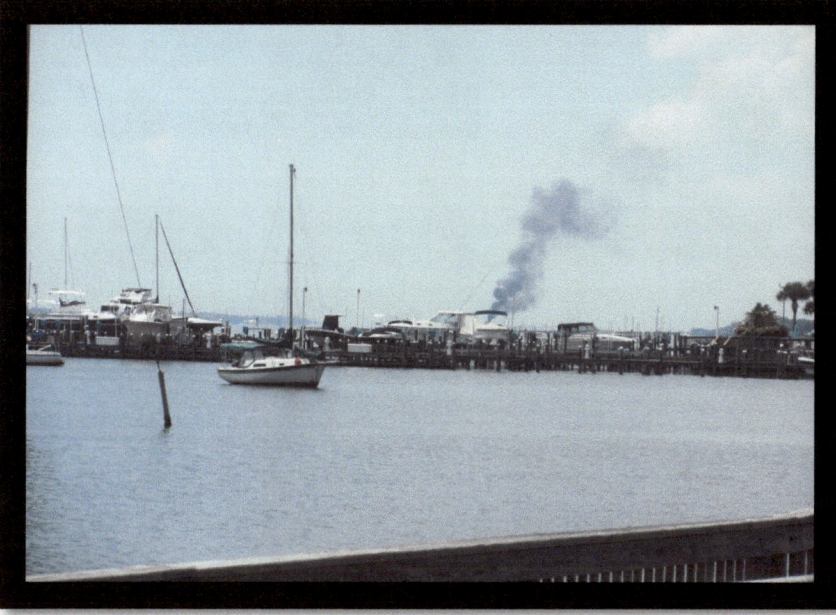

These pictures were taken by Loretta Morris –White, the Author, Editor and Publisher of this Magazine.

Back in 2010, Loretta had to leave her family and move into a Homeless Veteran Transitional Housing program in Brevard County, Florida. Being so far away from her family, she felt alone and confused. The only thing that she could physically do that allowed her to cope at that time in her life was to find the Beauty of it All.

So through the lens of her camera, her life changed.

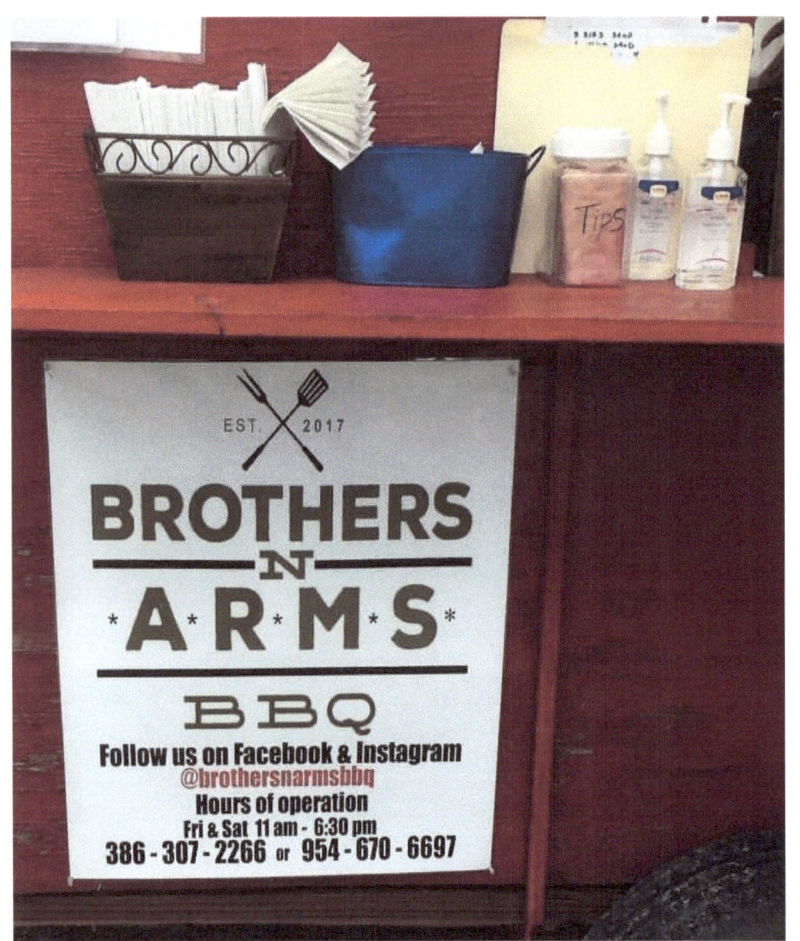

EST. 2017

BROTHERS N ARMS

BBQ

Follow us on Facebook & Instagram
@brothersnarmsbbq
Hours of operation
Fri & Sat 11 am - 6:30 pm
386 - 307 - 2266 or 954 - 670 - 6697

901 Mercy Drive Orlando, Florida

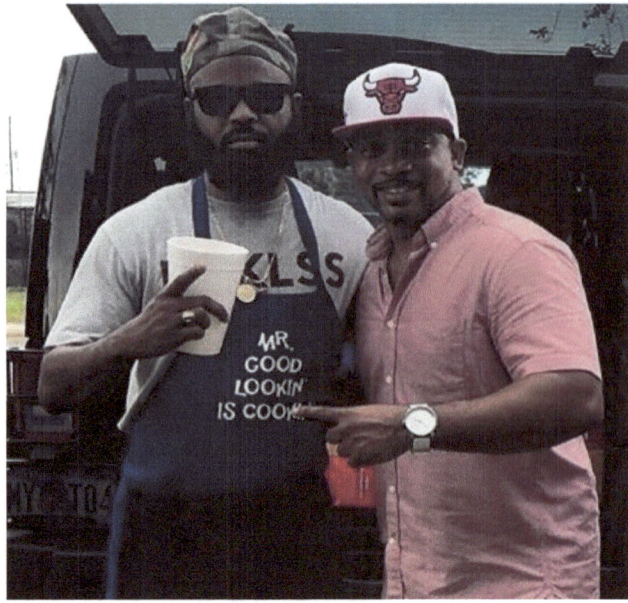

VETERAN OWNED

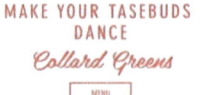

MAKE YOUR TASEBUDS DANCE
Collard Greens
MENU

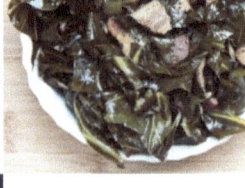

Mac and Cheese
MELTS IN YOUR MOUTH
MENU

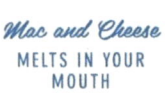

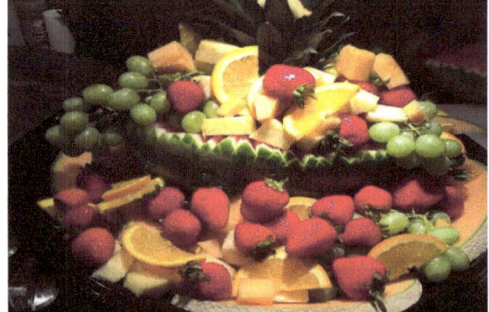

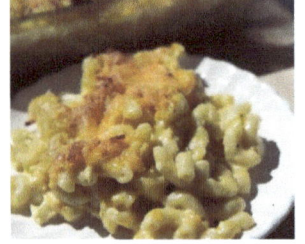

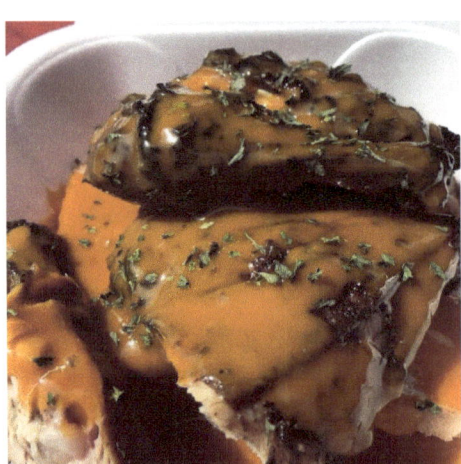

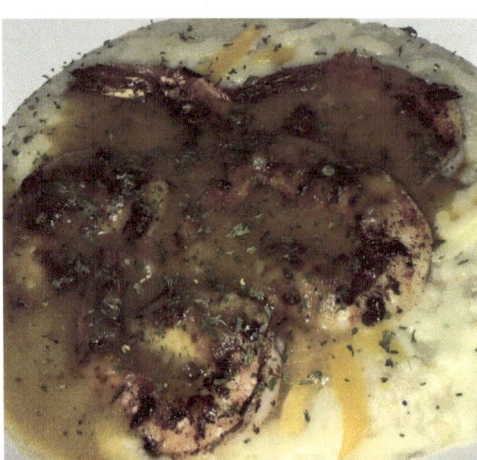

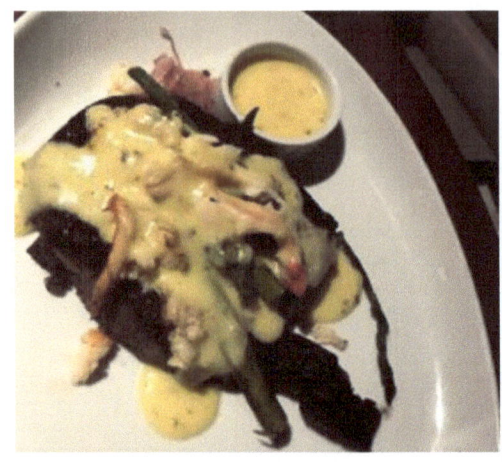

JAZZY ARTZ

ON ANOTHER NOTE...

Thank you for your support. Your Ads, Donations and Contributions will be supporting a Disabled Veteran.

100% Veteran Owned

Greetings once again,

I am a U.S. Army Veteran. I served this Country from 1979—1989. I enlisted one month after I graduated High School at the age of 17.

I served two European Tours, spending a total of 6 years overseas. While in the Military, I had two children. After being honorably discharged, I became a Homeless Veteran and having two more children. I was later diagnosed with chronic PTSD. I am still receiving treatment and therapy. In the meantime, while waiting for my Disability decision which has to this date, taken 7 years; I utilize my talents creating and enjoying the Arts.

I love promoting beauty and things that make me happy. Believe me, finances have been an awful challenge for me, and I have had to spend time in a hospital more times then I care to remember due to these crisis, but I refuse to give up.

My ultimate goal is to have an Art Gallery where Veterans and those that are unable to showcase their work anywhere else, can share their crafts. I also want to include a gift shop and book store for Independent, Self Published Authors, like myself. We might as well include a small Café so we can relax with some of the finest Teas, Coffees and pastries.

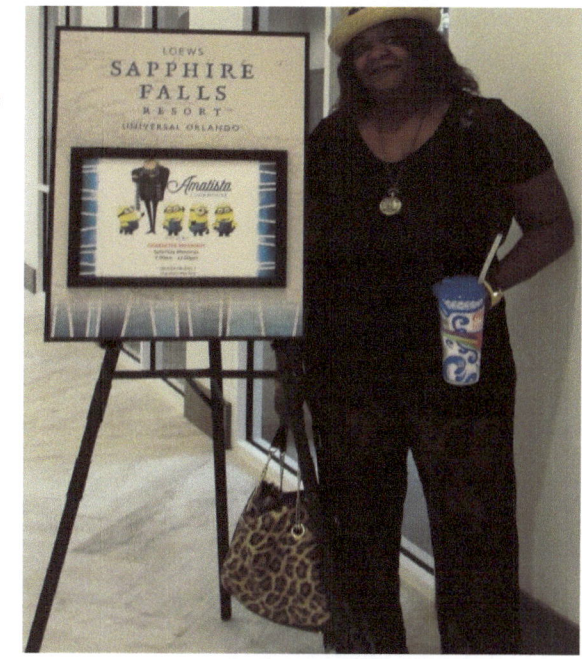

Now, if you are interested in my story after reading this note, believe me, I have the books. Check them out on Amazon. com

So, thank you all for your support.

mind your business

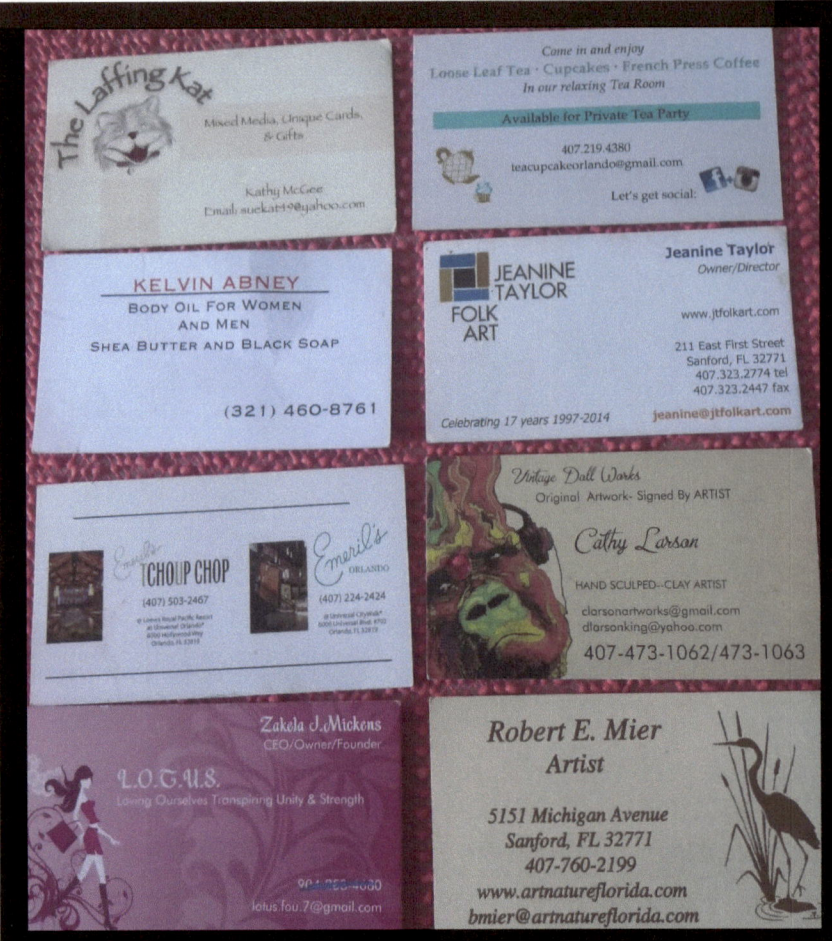

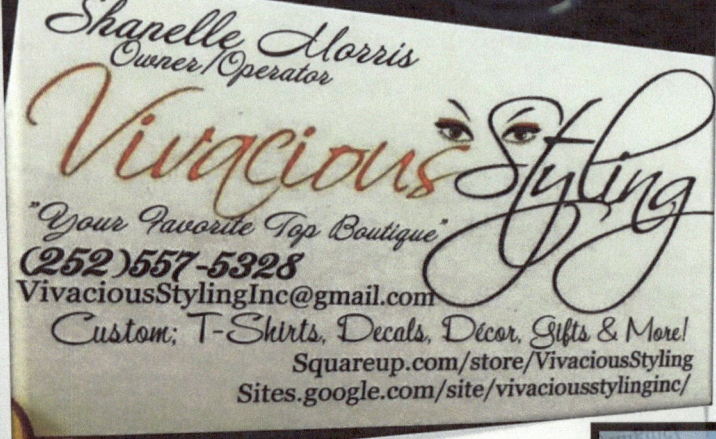

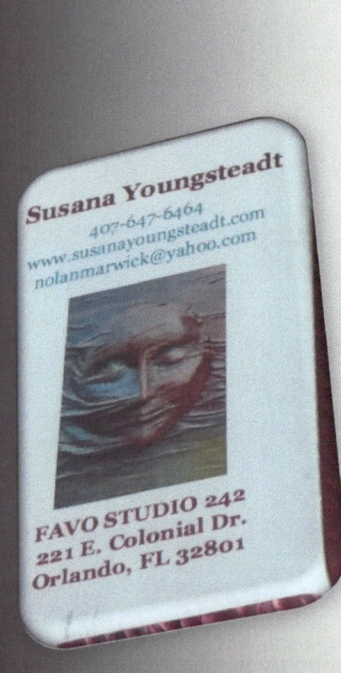

JUNE 2016, A TRAGEDY STRUCK THE PULSE NIGHT CLUB ORLANDO, FLORIDA HERE ARE THE 49 NAMES OF THE VICTIMS

#ORLANDOSTRONG

On June 12, 2016, a tragedy hit the Pulse Nightclub located two streets over from where I live. This situation seemed to have brought awareness around the world. The love was shared by all. No one saw race, creed, color, religion, gender or sexual orientation.

The only thing that was shared was hurt, pain and love for one another. Many shed tears, held vigils around the world, even many large Corporations.

Many people made it a point to stop by the Pulse Nightclub to place special gifts, flowers, and pray for those that were lost. It did not matter if we knew anyone that had been taken away from us or not, we grieved. Many also stopped by the site to show concern by signing the wall and taking pictures; now making the Pulse Nightclub a Historical site.

1. Stanley Almodovar III
2. Amanda Alvear
3. Oscar A. Aracena-Montero
4. RodolfoAyala-Ayala
5. Antonio Davon Brown
6. Darryl RomanBurt II
7. Angel L. Candelario-Padro
8. Juan Chevez-Martinez
9. Luis DanielConde
10. Cory James Connell
11. Tevin Eugene Crosby
12. Deonka Deidra Drayton
13. Simon Adrian
14. Carrillo Fernandez
15. Leroy Valentin Fernandez
16. Mercedez Marisol Flores
17. Peter O. Gonzalez-Cruz
18. Juan Ramon Guerrero
19. Paul Terrell Henry
20. Frank Hernandez

21. Miguel Angel Honorato
22. Javier Jorge-Reyes
23. Jason Benjamin Josaphat
24. Eddie Jamoldroy Justice
25. Anthony Luis Laureanodisla
26. Christopher Andrew Leinonen
27. Alejandro Barrios Martinez
28. Brenda Lee Marquez McCool
29. Gilberto Ramon
30. Silva Menedez
31. Kimberly Morris
32. Akyra Monet Murray
33. Luis Omar Ocasio-Capo
34. Geraldo A Ortiz-Jimenez
35. Eric Ivan Ortiz
36. Joel Rayon Paniagua
37. Jean Carlos Mendez Perez
38. Xavier E.S. Rosado
39. Christopher Joseph Sanfeliz
40. Yilmary Rodriguez Solivan

41. Edward Sotomayor Jr.
42. Shane Evan Tomlinson
43. Martin BenitezTorres
44. Jonathan A.C. Vega
45. Juan P.R. Velazquez
46. Luis S. Vielma
47. Franky J.D. Velazquez
48. Luis D.Wilson-Leon
49. Jerald Arthur Wright

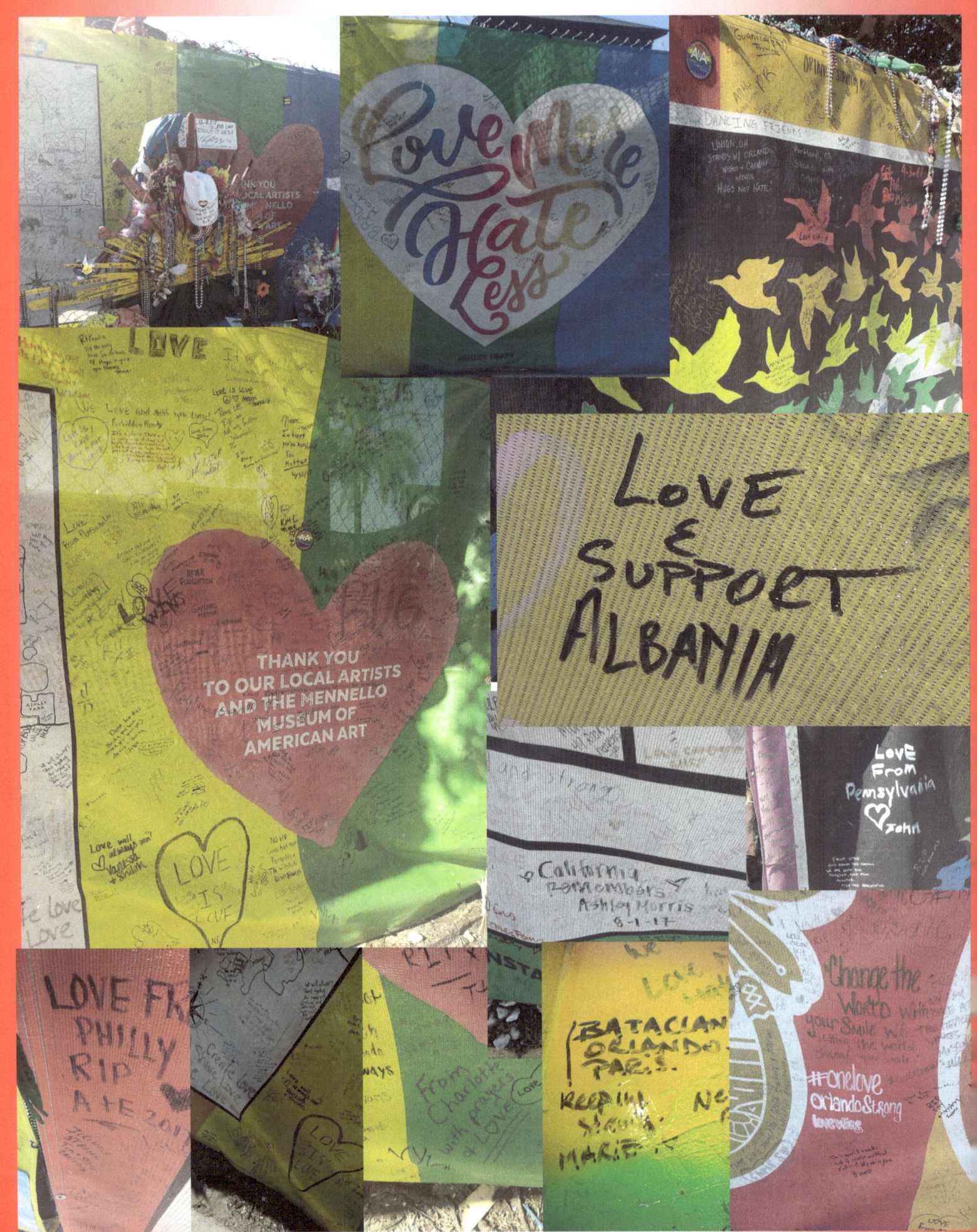

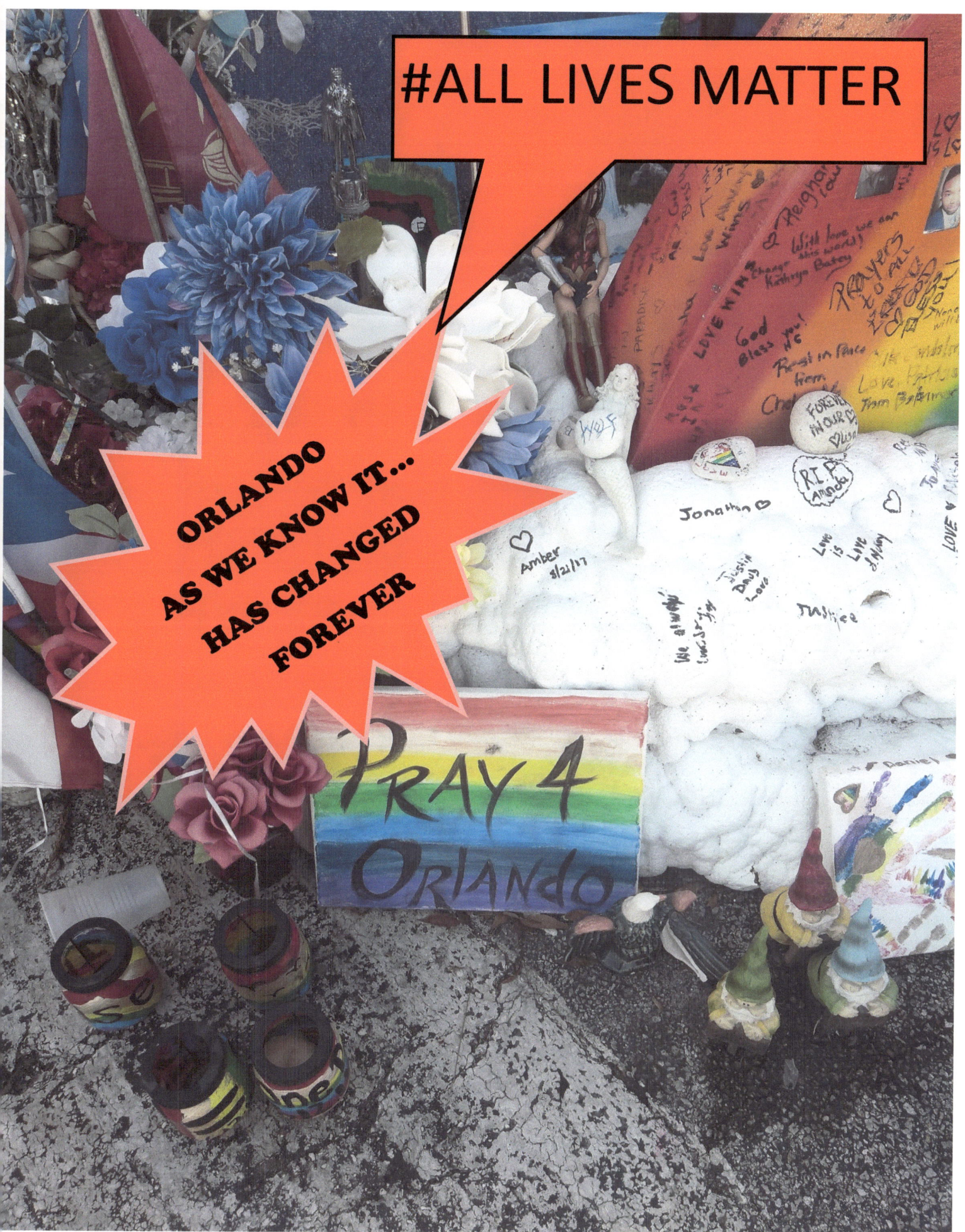